BITTER-SWEET.

BITTER-SWEET

A POEM.

BY

J. G. HOLLAND,

AUTHOR OF "THE BAY PATH," "TITCOMB'S LETTERS," ETC.

FIFTEENTH EDITION.

NEW YORK:
CHARLES SCRIBNER, 124 GRAND STREET
MDCCCLXIII.

CONTENTS.

PICTURE.

———o———

WINTER's wild birthnight! In the fretful East
The uneasy wind moans with its sense of cold,
And sends its sighs through gloomy mountain gorge,
Along the valley, up the whitening hill,
To tease the sighing spirits of the pines,
And waste in dismal woods their chilly life.
The sky is dark, and on the huddled leaves—
The restless, rustling leaves—sifts down its sleet,
Till the sharp crystals pin them to the earth,
And they grow still beneath the rising storm.
The roofless bullock hugs the sheltering stack,
With cringing head and closely gathered feet,
And waits with dumb endurance for the morn.
Deep in a gusty cavern of the barn

The witless calf stands blatant at his chain;
While the brute mother, pent within her stall,
With the wild stress of instinct goes distraught,
And frets her horns, and bellows through the night.
The stream runs black; and the far waterfall
That sang so sweetly through the summer eves,
And swelled and swayed to Zephyr's softest breath,
Leaps with a sullen roar the dark abyss,
And howls its hoarse responses to the wind.
The mill is still. The distant factory,
That swarmed yestreen with many-fingered life,
And bridged the river with a hundred bars
Of molten light, is dark, and lifts its bulk
With dim, uncertain angles, to the sky.

* * * * * *

Yet lower bows the storm. The leafless trees
Lash their lithe limbs, and, with majestic voice,
Call to each other through the deepening gloom;
And slender trunks that lean on burly boughs
Shriek with the sharp abrasion; and the oak,

Mellowed in fibre by unnumbered frosts,
Yields to the shoulder of the Titan Blast,
Forsakes its poise, and, with a booming crash,
Sweeps a fierce passage to the smothered rocks,
And lies a shattered ruin.

* * * * * * *

Other scene:—

Across the swale, half up the pine-capped hill,
Stands the old farm-house with its clump of barns—
The old red farm-house—dim and dun to-night,
Save where the ruddy firelights from the hearth
Flap their bright wings against the window panes,—
A billowy swarm that beat their slender bars,
Or seek the night to leave their track of flame
Upon the sleet, or sit, with shifting feet
And restless plumes, among the poplar boughs—
The spectral poplars, standing at the gate.

And now a man, erect, and tall, and strong,
Whose thin white hair, and cheeks of furrowed bronze,

And ancient dress, betray the patriarch,
Stands at the window, listening to the storm
And as the fire leaps with a wilder flame—
Moved by the wind—it wraps and glorifies
His stalwart frame, until it flares and glows
Like the old prophets, in transfigured guise,
That shape the sunset for cathedral aisles.
And now it passes, and a sweeter shape
Stands in its place. O blest maternity!
Hushed on her bosom, in a light embrace,
Her baby sleeps, wrapped in its long white robe;
And as the flame, with soft, auroral sweeps,
Illuminates the pair, how like they seem,
O Virgin Mother! to thyself and thine!
Now Samuel comes with curls of burning gold
To hearken to the voice of God without:
"Speak, mighty One! Thy little servant hears!"
And Miriam, maiden, from her household cares
Comes to the window in her loosened robe,—
Comes with the blazing timbrels in her hand,—

And, as the noise of winds and waters swells,
It shapes the song of triumph to her lips:
"The horse and he who rode are overthrown!"
And now a man of noble port and brow,
And aspect of benignant majesty,
Assumes the vacant niche, while either side
Press the fair forms of children, and I hear.
"Suffer the little ones to come to me!"

PERSONS

—o—

Here dwells the good old farmer, Israel,
In his ancestral home—a Puritan
Who reads his Bible daily, loves his God,
And lives serenely in the faith of Christ.
For three score years and ten his life has run
Through varied scenes of happiness and woe;
But, constant through the wide vicissitude,
He has confessed the giver of his joys,
And kissed the hand that took them; and whene'er
Bereavement has oppressed his soul with grief,
Or sharp misfortune stung his heart with pain,
He has bowed down in childlike faith, and said,

"Thy will, O God—thy will be done, not mine!"
His gentle wife, a dozen summers since,
Passed from his faithful arms and went to heaven;
And her best gift—a maiden sweetly named—
His daughter Ruth—orders the ancient house,
And fills her mother's place beside the board,
And cheers his life with songs and industry.
But who are these who crowd the house to-night—
A happy throng? Wayfaring pilgrims, who,
Grateful for shelter, charm the golden hours
With the sweet jargon of a festival?
Who are these fathers? who these mothers? who
These pleasant children, rude with health and joy?

It is the Puritan's Thanksgiving Eve;
And gathered home, from fresher homes around,
The old man's children keep the holiday—
In dear New England, since the fathers slept—
The sweetest holiday of all the year.
John comes with Prudence and her little girls,

And Peter, matched with Patience, brings his boys—
Fair boys and girls with good old Scripture names—
Joseph, Rebekah, Paul, and Samuel;
And Grace, young Ruth's companion in the house,
Till wrested from her last Thanksgiving Day
By the strong hand of Love, brings home her babe
And the tall poet David, at whose side
She went away. And seated in the midst,
Mary, a foster-daughter of the house,
Of alien blood—self-aliened many a year—
Whose chastened face and melancholy eyes
Bring all the wondering children to her knee,
Weeps with the strange excess of happiness,
And sighs with joy.

What recks the driving storm
Of such a scene as this? And what reck these
Of such a storm? For every heavy gust
That smites the windows with its cloud of sleet,
And shakes the sashes with its ghostly hands,

And rocks the mansion till the chimney's throat
Through all its sooty caverns shrieks and howls,
They give full bursts of careless merriment,
Or songs that send it baffled on its way.

PRELUDE.

---o---

DOUBT takes to wings on such a night as this;
And while the traveller hugs his fluttering cloak,
And staggers o'er the weary waste alone,
Beneath a pitiless heaven, they flap his face,
And wheel above, or hunt his fainting soul,
As, with relentless greed, a vulture throng,
With their lank shadows mock the glazing eyes
Of the last camel of the caravan.
And Faith takes forms and wings on such a night.
Where love burns brightly at the household hearth
And from the altar of each peaceful heart
Ascends the fragrant incense of its thanks,
And every pulse with sympathetic throb
Tells the true rhythm of trustfulest content,

They flutter in and out, and touch to smiles
The sleeping lips of infancy; and fan
The blush that lights the modest maiden's cheeks;
And toss the locks of children at their play.

Silence is vocal if we listen well;
And Life and Being sing in dullest ears
From morn to night, from night to morn again,
With fine articulations; but when God
Disturbs the soul with terror, or inspires
With a great joy, the words of Doubt and Faith
Sound quick and sharp like drops on forest leaves;
And we look up to where the pleasant sky
Kisses the thunder-caps, and drink the song.

A Song of Doubt

The day is quenched, and the sun is fled;
God has forgotten the world!
The moon is gone, and the stars are dead;
God has forgotten the world!

Evil has won in the horrid feud
  Of ages with The Throne ;
Evil stands on the neck of Good,
  And rules the world alone.

There is no good ; there is no God ,
  And Faith is a heartless cheat
Who bares the back for the Devil's rod,
  And scatters thorns for the feet.

What are prayers in the lips of death,
  Filling and chilling with hail ?
What are prayers but wasted breath
  Beaten back by the gale ?

The day is quenched, and the sun is fled ;
  God has forgotten the world !
The moon is gone and the stars are dead ;
  God has forgotten the world !

A Song of Faith.

Day will return with a fresher boon;
  God will remember the world!
Night will come with a newer moon;
  God will remember the world!

Evil is only the slave of Good;
  Sorrow the servant of Joy;
And the soul is mad that refuses food
  Of the meanest in God's employ.

The fountain of joy is fed by tears,
  And love is lit by the breath of sighs;
The deepest griefs and the wildest fears
  Have holiest ministries.

Strong grows the oak in the sweeping storm;
  Safely the flower sleeps under the snow;

And the farmer's hearth is never warm
  Till the cold wind starts to blow.

Day will return with a fresher boon;
  God will remember the world!
Night will come with a newer moon;
  God will remember the world!

FIRST MOVEMENT.

COLLOQUIAL.

FIRST MOVEMENT.

———o———

LOCALITY—*The square room of a New England farm-house.*

PRESENT—Israel, *head of the family;* John, Peter, David, Patience, Prudence, Grace, Mary, Ruth, *and* Children.

———o———

THE QUESTION STATED AND ARGUED.

ISRAEL.

Ruth, touch the cradle. Boys, you must be still!
The baby cannot sleep in such a noise.
Nay, Grace, stir not; she'll soothe him soon enough,
And tell him more sweet stuff in half an hour
Than you can dream, in dreaming half a year.

RUTH.

[*Kneeling and rocking the cradle*

What is the little one thinking about ?
Very wonderful things, no doubt.
Unwritten history !
Unfathomed mystery !
Yet he laughs and cries, and eats and drinks,
And chuckles and crows, and nods and winks,
As if his head were as full of kinks
And curious riddles as any sphinx !
Warped by colic, and wet by tears,
Punctured by pins, and tortured by fears,
Our little nephew will lose two years ;
And he'll never know
Where the summers go ;—
He need not laugh, for he'll find it so !

Who can tell what a baby thinks ?
Who can follow the gossamer links

By which the mannikin feels his way
Out from the shore of the great unknown,
Blind, and wailing, and alone,
Into the light of day ?—
Out from the shore of the unknown sea,
Tossing in pitiful agony,—
Of the unknown sea that reels and rolls,
Specked with the barks of little souls—
Barks that were launched on the other side,
And slipped from Heaven on an ebbing tide!
What does he think of his mother's eyes ?
What does he think of his mother's hair ?
What of the cradle-roof that flies
Forward and backward through the air ?
What does he think of his mother's breast—
Bare and beautiful, smooth and white,
Seeking it ever with fresh delight—
Cup of his life and couch of his rest ?
What does he think when her quick embrace
Presses his hand and buries his face

Deep where the heart-throbs sink and swell
With a tenderness she can never tell,
  Though she murmur the words
  Of all the birds—
Words she has learned to murmur well?
    Now he thinks he'll go to sleep!
    I can see the shadow creep
    Over his eyes, in soft eclipse,
    Over his brow, and over his lips,
    Out to his little finger-tips!
    Softly sinking, down he goes!
    Down he goes! Down he goes!

[*Rising and carefully retreating to her seat*

    See! He is hushed in sweet repose!

DAVID.

[*Yawning.*

Behold a miracle! Music transformed
To morphine, and the drowsy god invoked
By the poor prattle of a maiden's tongue:
A moment more, and we should all have gone

Down into dreamland with the babe! Ah, well!
There is no end of wonders.

RUTH.

None, indeed!
When lazy poets who have gorged themselves,
And cannot keep awake, make the attempt
To shift the burden of their drowsiness,
And charge a girl with what they owe to greed.

DAVID.

At your old tricks again! No sleep induced
By song of yours, or any other bird's,
Can linger long when you begin to talk.
Grace, box your sister's ears for me, and save
The trouble of my rising.

RUTH.

[Advancing and kneeling by the side of Grace

Sister mine.
Now give the proof of your obedience

To your imperious lord! Strike, if you dare!
I'll wake your baby if you lift your hand.
Ha! king; ha! poet; who is master now—
Baby or husband? Pr'ythee, tell me that.
Were I a man,—thank Heaven I am not!—
And had a wife who cared not for my will
More than your wife for yours, I'd hang myself,
Or wear an apron. See! she kisses me!

DAVID.

And answers to my will, though well she knows
I'll spare to her so terrible a task,
And take the awful burden on myself;
Which I will do, in future, if she please!

RUTH.

Now have you conquered! Look! I am your slave
Denounce me, scourge me, anything but kiss;
For life is sweet, and I alone am left
To comfort an old man.

ISRAEL.

Ruth, that will do!
Remember I'm a Justice of the Peace,
And bide no quarrels; and if you and David
Persist in strife, I'll place you under bonds
For good behavior, or condemn you both
To solitary durance for the night.

RUTH.

Father, you fail to understand the case,
And do me wrong. David has threatened me
With an assault that proves intent to kill;
And here's my sister Grace, his wedded wife,
Who'll take her oath, that just a year ago
He entered into bonds to keep the peace
Toward me and womankind.

DAVID.

I'm quite asleep.

ISRAEL.

We'll all agree, then, to pronounce it quits.

RUTH.

Till he awake again, of course. I trust
I have sufficient gallantry to grant
A nap between encounters, to a foe
With odds against him.

ISRAEL.

Peace, my daughter, peace!
You've had your full revenge, and we have had
Enough of laughter since the day began.
We must not squander all these precious hours
In jest and merriment; for when the sun
Shall rise to-morrow, we shall separate,
Not knowing we shall ever meet again.
Meetings like this are rare this side of Heaven,
And seem to me the best mementoes left
Of Eden's hours.

GRACE.

Most certainly the best,
And quite the rarest, but, unluckily,
The weakest, as we know ; for sin and pain
And evils multiform, that swarm the earth,
And poison all our joys and all our hearts,
Remind us most of Eden's forfeit bliss.

DAVID.

Forfeit through woman.

GRACE.

Forfeit through her power ;—
A power not lost, as most men know, I think,
Beyond the knowledge of their trustful wives.

MARY.

[*Rising, and walking hurriedly to the window*

'Tis a wild night without.

RUTH.

And getting wild
Within. Now, Grace, I—all of us—protest
Against a scene to-night. Look! You have driven
One to the window blushing, and your lord,
With lowering brow, is making stern essay
To stare the fire-dogs out of countenance.
These honest brothers, with their honest wives,
Grow glum and solemn, too, as if they feared
At the next gust to see the windows burst,
Or a riven poplar crashing through the roof.
And think of me!—a simple-hearted maid
Who learned from Cowper only yesterday
(Or a schoolmaster, with a handsome face,
And a strange passion for the text), the fact,
That wedded bliss alone survives the fall.
I'm shocked; I'm frightened; and I'll never wed
Unless I—change my mind!

ISRAEL.

And I consent.

DAVID.

And the schoolmaster with the handsome face
Propose.

RUTH.

Your pardon, father, for the jest!
But I have never patience with the ills
That make intrusion on my happy hours.
I know the world is full of evil things,
And shudder with the consciousness. I know
That care has iron crowns for many brows;
That Calvaries are everywhere, whereon
Virtue is crucified, and nails and spears
Draw guiltless blood; that sorrow sits and drinks
At sweetest hearts, till all their life is dry;
That gentle spirits on the rack of pain

Grow faint or fierce, and pray and curse by turns;
That Hell's temptations, clad in Heavenly guise
And armed with might, lie evermore in wait
Along life's path, giving assault to all—
Fatal to most; that Death stalks through the earth,
Choosing his victims, sparing none at last;
That in each shadow of a pleasant tree
A grief sits sadly sobbing to its leaves;
And that beside each fearful soul there walks
The dim, gaunt phantom of uncertainty,
Bidding it look before, where none may see,
And all must go; but I forget it all—
I thrust it from me always when I may;
Else I should faint with fear, or drown myself
In pity. God forgive me! but I've thought
A thousand times that if I had His power,
Or He my love, we'd have a different world
From this we live in.

ISRAEL.

Those are sinful thoughts,
My daughter, and too surely indicate
A wilful soul, unreconciled to God.

RUTH.

So you have told me often. You have said
That God is just, and I have looked around
To seek the proof in human lot, in vain.
The rain falls kindly on the just man's fields,
But on the unjust man's more kindly still;
And I have never known the winter's blast,
Or the quick lightning, or the pestilence,
Make nice discriminations when let slip
From God's right hand.

ISRAEL.

'Tis a great mystery;
Yet God is just, and,—blessed be His name!

Is loving too. I know that I am weak,
And that the pathway of His Providence
Is on the hills where I may never climb.
Therefore my reason yields her hand to Faith,
And follows meekly where the angel leads.
I see the rich man have his portion here;
And Lazarus, in glorified repose,
Sleep like a jewel on the breast of Faith
In Heaven's broad light. I see that whom God loves
He chastens sorely, but I ask not why.
I only know that God is just and good:
All else is mystery. Why evil lives
Within His universe, I may not know.
I know it lives, and taints the vital air;
And that in ways inscrutable to me—
Yet compromising not his soundless love
And boundless power—it lives against His will.

RUTH.

I am not satisfied. If evil live
Against God's will, evil is king of all,
And they do well who worship Lucifer.
I am not satisfied. My reason spurns
Such prostitution to absurdities.
I know that you are happy; but I shrink
From your blind faith with loathing and with fear.
And feel that I must win it, if I win,
With the surrender, not of will alone,
But of the noblest faculty that God
Has crowned me with.

ISRAEL.

O blind and stubborn child!
My light, my joy, my burden and my grief!
How would I lead you to the wells of peace,
And see you dip your fevered palms and drink!
Gladly to purchase this would I lay down

The precious remnant of my life, and sleep,
Wrapped in the faith you spurn, till the archangel
Sounds the last trump. But God's good will be done!
I leave you with Him.

RUTH.

Father, talk not thus!
Oh, do not blame me! I would do it all,
If but to bless you with a single joy;
But I am helpless.

ISRAEL.

God will help you, Ruth.

RUTH.

To quench my reason? Can I ask the boon?
My lips would blister with the blasphemy.
I cannot take your faith; and that is why
I would forget that I am in a world

Where evil lives, and why I guard my joys
With such a jealous care.

DAVID.

There, Ruth, sit down!
'Tis the old question, with the old reply.
You fly along the path, with bleeding feet,
Where many feet have flown and bled before;
And he who seeks to guide you to the goal,
Has (let me say it, father,) stopped far short,
And taken refuge at a wayside inn,
Whose haunted halls and mazy passages
Receive no light, save through the riddled roof,
Pierced thick by pilgrim staves, that Faith may lie
Upon its back, and only gaze on Heaven.
I would not banish evil if I could;
Nor would I be so deep in love with joy
As to seek for it in forgetfulness,
Through faith or fear.

RUTH.

Teach me the better way,
And every expiration from my lips
Shall be a grateful blessing on your head;
And in the coming world I'll seek the side
Of no more gracious angel than the man
Who gives me brotherhood by leading me
Home with himself to heaven.

ISRAEL.

My son,
Be careful of your words! 'Tis no light thing
To take the guidance of a straying soul.

DAVID.

I mark the burden well, and love it, too,
Because I love the girl and love her lord,
And seek to vindicate His love to her
And waken hers for Him. Be this my plea:

God is almighty—all-benevolent;
And naught exists save by His loving will.
Evil, or what we reckon such, exists,
And not against His will; else the Supreme
Is subject, and we have in place of God
A phantom nothing, with a phantom name.
Therefore I care not whether He ordain
That evil live, or whether He permit;
Therefore I ask not why, in either case,
As if He meant to curse me, but I ask
What He would have this evil do for me?
What is its mission? what its ministry?
What golden fruit lies hidden in its husk?
How shall it nurse my virtue, nerve my will,
Chasten my passions, purify my love,
And make me in some goodly sense like Him
Who bore the cross of evil while He lived,
Who hung and bled upon it when He died,
And now, in glory, wears the victor's crown?

ISRAEL.

If evil, then, have privilege and part
In the economy of holiness,
Why came the Christ to save us from its power
And bring us restoration of the bliss
Lost in the lapse of Eden?

DAVID.

And would you
Or Ruth have restoration of that bliss,
And welcome transplantation to the state
Associate with it?

RUTH.

Would I? Would I not!
Oh, I have dreamed of it a thousand times,
Sleeping and waking, since the torch of thought
Flashed into flame at Revelation's touch,
And filled my spirit with its quenchless fire.

Most envious dreams of innocence and joy
Have haunted me,—dreams that were born in sin,
Yet swathed in stainless snow. I've dreamed, and dreamed,
Of wondrous trees, crowned with perennial green,
Whose soft still shadows gleamed with golden lamps
Of pensile fruitage, or were flushed with life
Radiant and tuneful when broad flocks of birds
Swept in and out like sheets of living flame.
I've dreamed of aisles tufted with velvet grass,
And bordered with the strange intelligence
Of myriad loving eyes among the flowers,
That watched me with a curious, calm delight,
As rows of wayside cherubim may watch
A new soul, walking into Paradise.
I've dreamed of sunsets when the sun supine
Lay rocking on the ocean like a god,
And threw his weary arms far up the sky,
And with vermillion-tinted fingers toyed
With the long tresses of the evening star.

I've dreamed of dreams more beautiful than all—
Dreams that were music, perfume, vision, bliss,—
Blent and sublimed, till I have stood enwrapped
In the quick essence of an atmosphere
That made me tremble to unclose my eyes
Lest I should look on God. And I have dreamed
Of sinless men and maids, mated in heaven,
Ere yet their souls had sought for beauteous forms
To give them human sense and residence,
Moving through all this realm of choice delights
For ever and for aye; with hands and hearts
Immaculate as light; without a thought
Of evil, and without a name for fear.
Oh, when I wake from happy dreams like these,
To the old consciousness that I must die,
To the old presence of a guilty heart,
To the old fear that haunts me night and day,
Why should I not deplore the graceless fall
That makes me what I am, and shuts me out
From a condition and society

As much above a sinful maiden's dreams
As Eden blest surpasses Eden curst?

DAVID.

So you would be another Eve, and so—
Fall with the first temptation, like herself!
God seeks for virtue; you for innocence.
You'll find it in the cradle—nowhere else—
Save in your dreams, among the grown up babes
That dwelt in Eden—powerless, pulpy souls
That showed a dimple for each touch of sin.
God seeks for virtue, and, that it may live,
It must resist, and that which it resists
Must live. Believe me, God has other thought
Than restoration of our fallen race
To its primeval innocence and bliss.
If Jesus Christ—as we are taught—was slain
From the foundation of the world, it was
Because our evil lived in essence then—
Coeval with the great, mysterious fact.

And He was slain that we might be transformed,—
Not into Adam's sweet similitude—
But the more glorious image of Himself,—
A resolution of our destiny
As high transcending Eden's life and lot
As he surpasses Eden's fallen lord.

RUTH.

You're very bold, my brother, very bold.
Did I not know you for an earnest man,
When sacred themes move you to utterance,
I'd chide you for those most irreverent words
Which make essential to the Christian scheme
That which the scheme was made to kill, or cure.

DAVID.

Yet they do save some very awkward words,
That limp to make apology for God,
And, while they justify Him, half confess
The adverse verdict of appearances.

I am ashamed that in this Christian age
The pious throng still hug the fallacy
That this dear world of ours was not ordained
The theatre of evil; for no law
Declared of God from all eternity
Can live a moment save by lease of pain.
Law cannot live, e'en in God's inmost thought,
Save by the side of evil. What were law
But a weak jest without its penalty?
Never a law was born that did not fly
Forth from the bosom of Omnipotence
Matched, wing-and-wing, with evil and with good,
Avenger and rewarder—both of God.

RUTH.

I face your thought and give it audience;
But I cannot embrace it till it come
With some of truth's credentials in its hands—
The fruits of gracious ministries.

DAVID.

Does he
Who, driven to labor by the threat'ning weeds,
And forced to give his acres light and air
And traps for dew and reservoirs for rain,
Till, in the smoky light of harvest time,
The ragged husks reveal the golden corn,
Ask truth's credentials of the weeds? Does he
Who prunes the orchard boughs, or tills the field,
Or fells the forests, or pursues their prey,
Until the gnarly muscles of his limbs
And the free blood that thrills in all his veins
Betray the health that toil alone secures,
Ask truth's credentials at the hand of toil?
Do you ask truth's credentials of the storm
Which, while we entertain communion here,
Makes better music for our huddling hearts
Than choirs of stars can sing in fairest nights?
Yet weeds are evils—evils toil and storm.

We may suspect the fair, smooth face of good;
But evil, that assails us undisguised,
Bears evermore God's warrant in its hands.

ISRAEL.

I fear these silver sophistries of yours.
If my poor judgment gives them honest weight,
Far less than thirty will betray your Lord.
You call that evil which is good, and good
That which is evil. You apologize
For that which God must hate, and justify
The life and perpetuity of that
Which sets itself against His holiness,
And sends its discords through the universe

DAVID.

I sorrrow if I shock you, for I seek
To comfort and inspire. I see around
A silent company of doubtful souls;
But I may challenge any one of them

To quote the meanest blessing of its life,
And prove that evil did not make the gift,
Or bear it from the giver to its hands.
The great salvation wrought by Jesus Christ—
That sank an Adam to reveal a God—
Had never come, but at the call of sin.
No risen Lord could eat the feast of love
Here on the earth, or yonder in the sky,
Had He not lain within the sepulchre.
'Tis not the lightly laden heart of man
That loves the best the hand that blesses all;
But that which, groaning with its weight of sin,
Meets with the mercy that forgiveth much.
God never fails in an experiment,
Nor tries experiment upon a race
But to educe its highest style of life,
And sublimate its issues. Thus to me
Evil is not a mystery, but a means
Selected from the infinite resource
To make the most of me.

RUTH.

Thank God for light!
These truths are slowly dawning on my soul,
And take position in the firmament
That spans my thought, like stars that know their
place.
Dear Lord! what visions crowd before my eyes—
Visions drawn forth from memory's mysteries
By the sweet shining of these holy lights!
I see a girl, once lightest in the dance,
And maddest with the gayety of life,
Grow pale and pulseless, wasting day by day,
While death lies idly dreaming in her breast,
Blighting her breath, and poisoning her blood.
I see her frantic with a fearful thought
That haunts and horrifies her shrinking soul,
And bursts in sighs and sobs and feverish prayers;
And now, at last, the awful struggle ends.
A sweet smile sits upon her angel face,

And peace, with downy bosom, nestles close
Where her worn heart throbs faintly; closer still
As the death shadows gather; closer still,
As, on white wings, the outward-going soul
Flies to a home it never would have sought,
Had a great evil failed to point the way.
I see a youth whom God has crowned with power
And cursed with poverty. With bravest heart
He struggles with his lot, through toilsome years,—
Kept to his task by daily want of bread,
And kept to virtue by his daily task,—
Till, gaining manhood in the manly strife,—
The fire that fills him smitten from a flint—
The strength that arms him wrested from a fiend—
He stands, at last, a master of himself,
And, in that grace, a master of his kind.

DAVID.

Familiar visions these, but ever full
Of inspiration and significance.

Now that your eyes are opened and you see,
Your heart should take swift cognizance, and feel.
How do these visions move you?

RUTH.

Like the hand
Of a strong angel on my shoulder laid,
Touching the secret of the spirit's wings.
My heart grows brave. I'm ready now to work—
To work with God, and suffer with His Christ;
Adopt His measures, and abide His means.
If, in the law that spans the universe
(The law its maker may not disobey),
Virtue may only grow from innocence
Through a great struggle with opposing ill;
If I must win my way to perfectness
In the sad path of suffering, like Him
The over-flowing river of whose life
Touches the flood-mark of humanity
On the white pillars of the heavenly throne,

Then welcome evil! Welcome sickness, toil,
Sorrow and pain, the fear and fact of death!

ISRAEL.

And welcome sin?

RUTH.

Ah, David! welcome sin?

DAVID.

The fact of sin—so much;—it must needs be
Offences come; if woe to him by whom,
Then with good reason; but the fact of sin
Unlocked the door to highest destiny,
That Christ might enter in and lead the way.
God loves not sin, nor I; but in the throng
Of evils that assail us, there are none
That yield their strength to Virtue's struggling arm
With such munificent reward of power
As great temptations. We may win by toil

Endurance; saintly fortitude by pain;
By sickness, patience; faith and trust by fear;
But the great stimulus that spurs to life,
And crowds to generous development
Each chastened power and passion of the soul,
Is the temptation of the soul to sin,
Resisted, and re-conquered, evermore.

RUTH.

I am content; and now that I have caught
Bright glimpses of the outlines of your scheme,
As of a landscape, graded to the sky,
And seen through trees while passing, I desire
No vision further till I make survey
In some good time when I may come alone,
And drink its beauty and its blessedness.
I've been forgetful in my earnestness,
And wearied every one with talk. These boys
Are restive grown, or nodding in their chairs,
And older heads are set, as if for sleep.

I beg their pardon for my theft of time,
And will offend no more.

DAVID.

Ruth, is it right
To leave a brother in such plight as this—
Either to imitate your courtesy,
Or by your act to be adjudged a boor?

RUTH.

Heaven grant you never note a sin of mine
Save of your own construction!

ISRAEL.

Let it pass!
I see the spell of thoughtfulness is gone,
Or going swiftly. I will not complain;
But ere these lads are fastened to their games,
And thoughts arise discordant with our theme,
Let us with gratitude approach the throne

And worship God. I wish once more to lead
Your hearts in prayer, and follow with my own
The leading of your song of thankfulness.
Then will I lease and leave you for the night
To such divertisement as suits the time,
And meets your humor.

[*They all arise and the old man prays.*

RUTH.

[*After a pause.*

David, let us see
Whether your memory prove as true as mine.
Do you recall the promise made by you
This night one year ago,—to write a hymn
For this occasion?

DAVID.

I recall, and keep.
Here are the copies, written fairly out.
Here,—father, Mary, Ruth, and all the rest;
There's one for each. Now what shall be the tune?

ISRAEL.

The old One Hundredth—noblest tune of tunes!
Old tunes are precious to me as old paths
In which I wandered when a happy boy.
In truth, they are the old paths of my soul,
Oft trod, well worn, familiar, up to God.

The Hymn.

[*In which all unite to sing*

For Summer's bloom and Autumn's blight,
For bending wheat and blasted maize,
For health and sickness, Lord of light,
And Lord of darkness, hear our praise!

We trace to Thee our joys and woes,—
To Thee of causes still the cause,—
We thank Thee that Thy hand bestows;
We bless Thee that Thy love withdraws.

We bring no sorrows to Thy throne;
  We come to Thee with no complaint;
In Providence Thy will is done,
  And that is sacred to the saint.

Here on this blest Thanksgiving Night;
  We raise to Thee our grateful voice;
For what Thou doest, Lord, is right;
  And thus believing, we rejoice.

GRACE.

A good old tune, indeed, and strongly sung;
But, in my mind, the man who wrote the hymn
Had seemed more modest, had he paused awhile,
Ere by a trick he furnished other tongues
With words he only has the heart to sing.

DAVID.

Oh, Grace! Dear Grace!

RUTH.

You may well cry for grace,
If that's the company you have to keep.

GRACE.

I thought you convert to his sophistry.
It makes no difference to him, you know,
Whether I plague or please.

RUTH.

It does to you.

ISRAEL.

There, children! No more bitter words like those!
I do not understand them; they awake
A sad uneasiness within my heart.
I found but Christian meaning in the hymn;
Aye, I could say *amen* to every line,
As to the breathings of my own poor prayer.
But let us talk no more. I'll to my bed.
Good night, my children! Happy thoughts be yours
Till sleep arrive—then happy dreams till dawn!

ALL.

Father, good night!

[ISRAEL *retires.*

RUTH.

There, little boys and girls—
Off to the kitchen! Now there's fun for you.
Play blind-man's-buff until you break your heads;
And then sit down beside the roaring fire,
And with wild stories scare yourselves to death.
We'll all be out there, by-and-by. Meanwhile,
I'll try the cellar; and if David, here,
Will promise good behavior, he shall be
My candle-bearer, basket-bearer, and—
But no! The pitcher I will bear myself.
I'll never trust a pitcher to a man
Under this house, and—seventy years of age.

[*The children rush out of the room with a shout, which wakes the baby.*

That noisy little youngster on the floor
Slept through theology, but wakes with mirth—

Precocious little creature! He must go
Up to his chamber. Come, Grace, take him off,—
Basket and all. Mary will lend a hand,
And keep you company until he sleeps.

[GRACE *and* MARY *remove the cradle to the chamber, and* DAVID *and* RUTH *retire to the cellar.*

JOHN.

[*Rising and yawning.*

Isn't she the strangest girl you ever saw?

PRUDENCE.

Queer, rather, I should say. Grace, now, is strange.
I think she treats her husband shamefully.
I can't imagine what possesses her,
Thus to toss taunts at him with every word.
If in his doctrines there be truth enough,
He'll be a saint.

PATIENCE.

If he live long enough.

JOHN.

Well, now I tell you, such wild men as he,—
Men who have crazy crotchets in their heads,—
Can't make a woman happy. Don't you see?
He isn't settled. He has wandered off
From the old landmarks, and has lost himself.
I may judge wrongly; but if truth were told
There'd be excuse for Grace, I warrant ye.
Grace is a right good girl, or was, before
She married David.

PATIENCE.

Everybody says
He makes provision for his family,
Like a good husband.

PETER.

We can hardly tell.
When men get loose in their theology
The screws are started up in everything.

Of course, I don't apologize for Grace.
I think she might have done more prudently
Than introduce her troubles here to night,
But, after all, we do not know the cause
That stirs her fretfulness.

Well, let it go!
What does the evening's talk amount to? Who
Is wiser for the wisdom of the hour?
The good old paths are good enough for me.
The fathers walked to heaven in them, and we,
By following meekly where they trod, may reach
The home they found. There will be mysteries;
Let those who like, bother their heads with them
If Ruth and David seek to fathom all,
I wish them patience in their bootless quest.
For one, I'm glad the misty talk is done,
And we, alone.

PATIENCE.

And I.

JOHN.

I, too.

PRUDENCE.

And I.

FIRST EPISODE.

———o———

LOCALITY—*The Cellar Stairs and the Cellar.*

PRESENT—DAVID *and* RUTH.

———o———

THE QUESTION ILLUSTRATED BY NATURE.

RUTH.

LOOK where you step, or you'll stumble!
  Care for your coat, or you'll crock it!
Down with your crown, man! Be humble!
  Put your head into your pocket,
  Else something or other will knock it.
Don't hit that jar of cucumbers

Standing on the broad stair!
They have not waked from their slumbers
Since they stood there.

DAVID.

Yet they have lived in a constant jar!
What remarkable sleepers they are!

RUTH.

Turn to the left—shun the wall—
One step more—that is all!
Now we are safe on the ground
I will show you around.

Sixteen barrels of cider
Ripening all in a row!
Open the vent-channels wider.
See the froth, drifted like snow,

Blown by the tempest below!
Those delectable juices
Flowed through the sinuous sluices
Of sweet springs under the orchard;
Climbed into fountains that chained them;
Dripped into cups that retained them,
And swelled till they dropped, and we gained them.
Then they were gathered and tortured
By passage from hopper to vat,
And fell—every apple crushed flat.
Ah! how the bees gathered round them,
And how delicious they found them!
Oat-straw, as fragrant as clover,
Was platted, and smoothly turned over,
Weaving a neatly-ribbed basket;
And, as they built up the casket,
In went the pulp by the scoop-full,
Till the juice flowed by the stoup-full,—
Filling the half of a puncheon
While the men swallowed their luncheon.

Pure grew the stream with the stress
  Of the lever and screw,
Till the last drops from the press
  Were as bright as the dew.
There were these juices spilled;
There were these barrels filled;
Sixteen barrels of cider—
Ripening all in a row!
Open the vent-channels wider!
See the froth, drifted like snow,
Blown by the tempest below!

DAVID.

Hearts, like apples, are hard and sour,
Till crushed by Pain's resistless power;
And yield their juices rich and bland
To none but Sorrow's heavy hand.
The purest streams of human love
  Flow naturally never,

But gush by pressure from above,
  With God's hand on the lever.
The first are turbidest and meanest;
The last are sweetest and serenest.

RUTH.

Sermon quite short for the text!
What shall we hit upon next?
Lift up the lid of that cask;
  See if the brine be abundant;
Easy for me were the task
  To make it redundant
With tears for my beautiful Zephyr—
  Pet of the pasture and stall—
Whitest and comeliest heifer,
  Gentlest of all!
  Oh, it seemed cruel to slay her!
  But they insulted my prayer
  For her careless and innocent life,

And the creature was brought to the knife
With gratitude in her eye;
For they patted her back, and chafed her head,
And coaxed her with softest words, as they led
Her up to the ring to die.
Do you blame me for crying
When my Zephyr was dying?
I shut my room and my ears,
And opened my heart and my tears,
And wept for the half of a day;
And I could not go
To the rooms below
Till the butcher went away.

DAVID.

Life evermore is fed by death,
In earth and sea and sky;
And, that a rose may breathe its breath,
Something must die.

Earth is a sepulchre of flowers,
Whose vitalizing mould
Through boundless transmutation towers,
In green and gold.

The oak tree, struggling with the blast,
Devours its father tree,
And sheds its leaves and drops its mast,
That more may be.

The falcon preys upon the finch,
The finch upon the fly
And nought will loose the hunger-pinch
But death's wild cry.

The milk-haired heifer's life must pass
That it may fill your own,
As passed the sweet life of the grass
She fed upon.

The power enslaved by yonder cask
  Shall many burdens bear;
Shall nerve the toiler at his task,
          The soul at prayer.

From lowly woe springs lordly joy;
  From humbler good diviner;
The greater life must aye destroy
          And drink the minor.

From hand to hand life's cup is passed
  Up Being's piled gradation,
Till men to angels yield at last
          The rich collation.

RUTH.

Well, we are done with the brute;
Now let us look at the fruit,—
Every barrel, I'm told,
From grafts half a dozen years old.

That is a barrel of russets;
But we can hardly discuss its
  Spheres of frost and flint,
Till, smitten by thoughts of Spring,
And the old tree blossoming,
Their bronze takes a yellower tint,
And the pulp grows mellower in't.
But oh! when they're sick with the savors
  Of sweets that they dream of,
Sure, all the toothsomest flavors
  They hold the cream of!
You will be begging in May,
In your irresistible way,
For a peck of the apples in gray.

Those are the pearmains, I think,—
Bland and insipid as eggs;
They were too lazy to drink
  The light to its dregs,
And left them upon the rind—

A delicate film of blue—
Leave them alone;—I can find
Better apples for you.

Those are the Rhode Island greenings;
Excellent apples for pies;
There are no mystical meanings
  In fruit of that color and size.
They are too coarse and too juiceful;
They are too large and too useful.

There are the Baldwins and Flyers,
Wrapped in their beautiful fires!
Color forks up from their stems
  As if painted by Flora,
Or as out from the pole stream the flames
  Of the Northern Aurora.

Here shall our quest have a close;
Fill up your basket with those;

Bite through their vesture of flame,
And then you will gather
All that is meant by the name,
"Seek-no-farther!"

DAVID.

The native orchard's fairest trees,
Wild springing on the hill,
Bear no such precious fruits as these,
And never will;

Till axe and saw and pruning knife
Cut from them every bough,
And they receive a gentler life
Than crowns them now.

And Nature's children, evermore,
Though grown to stately stature,
Must bear the fruit their fathers bore—
The fruit of nature;

Till every thrifty vice is made
  The shoulder for a cion,
Cut from the bending trees that shade
      The hills of Zion.

Sorrow must crop each passion-shoot,
  And pain each lust infernal,
Or human life can bear no fruit
      To life eternal.

For angels wait on Providence;
  And mark the sundered places,
To graft with gentlest instruments
      The heavenly graces.

RUTH.

Well, you're a curious creature!
You should have been a preacher.
  But look at that bin of potatoes—

Grown in all singular shapes—
Red and in clusters, like grapes,
  Or more like tomatoes.
Those are Merinoes, I guess;
  Very prolific and cheap;
They make an excellent mess
  For a cow, or a sheep,
And are good for the table, they say,
When the winter has passed away.

Those are my beautiful Carters;
Every one doomed to be martyrs
  To the eccentric desire
Of Christian people to skin them,—
  Brought to the trial of fire
For the good that is in them!
Ivory tubers—divide one!
  Ivory all the way through!
Never a hollow inside one;
  Never a core, black or blue!

Ah, you should taste them when roasted!
  (Chestnuts are not half so good;)
And you would find that I've boasted
  Less than I should.
They make the meal for Sunday noon;
  And, if ever you eat one, let me beg
  You to manage it just as you do an egg.
Take a pat of butter, a silver spoon,
And wrap your napkin round the shell:
Have you seen a humming-bird probe the bell
Of a white-lipped morning-glory?
Well, that's the rest of the story!
But it's very singular, surely,
They should produce so poorly.
Father knows that I want them,
So he continues to plant them;
But, if I try to argue the question,
  He scoffs, as a thrifty farmer will;
And puts me down with the stale suggestion—
  "Small potatoes, and few in a hill."

DAVID.

Thus is it over all the earth!
That which we call the fairest,
And prize for its surpassing worth,
Is always rarest.

Iron is heaped in mountain piles,
And gluts the laggard forges;
But gold-flakes gleam in dim defiles
And lonely gorges.

The snowy marble flecks the land
With heaped and rounded ledges,
But diamonds hide within the sand
Their starry edges.

The finny armies clog the twine
That sweeps the lazy river,
But pearls come singly from the brine,
With the pale diver.

God gives no value unto men
  Unmatched by meed of labor;
And Cost of Worth has ever been
  The closest neighbor.

Wide is the gate and broad the way
  That open to perdition,
And countless multitudes are they
  Who seek admission.

But strait the gate, the path unkind,
  That lead to life immortal,
And few the careful feet that find
  The hidden portal.

All common good has common price;
  Exceeding good, exceeding;
Christ bought the keys of Paradise
  By cruel bleeding;

And every soul that wins a place
  Upon its hills of pleasure,

Must give its all, and beg for grace
To fill the measure.

Were every hill a precious mine,
And golden all the mountains;
Were all the rivers fed with wine
By tireless fountains;

Life would be ravished of its zest,
And shorn of its ambition,
And sink into the dreamless rest
Of inanition.

Up the broad stairs that Value rears
Stand motives beck'ning earthward,
To summon men to nobler spheres,
And lead them worthward.

RUTH.

I'm afraid to show you anything more;
For parsnips and art are so very long,

That the passage back to the cellar-door
  Would be through a mile of song.
But Truth owns me for an honest teller;
  And, if the honest truth be told,
I am indebted to you and the cellar
  For a lesson and a cold.
And one or the other cheats my sight;
  (O silly girl! for shame!)
Barrels are hooped with rings of light,
  And stopped with tongues of flame.
Apples have conquered original sin,
  Manna is pickled in brine,
Philosophy fills the potato bin,
  And cider will soon be wine.
So crown the basket with mellow fruit,
  And brim the pitcher with pearls;
And we'll see how the old-time dainties suit
  The old-time boys and girls.

[*They ascend the stairs.*

SECOND MOVEMENT.

---o---

NARRATIVE.

SECOND MOVEMENT.

———o———

LOCALITY—*A Chamber.*

PRESENT—GRACE, MARY, *and the* BABY.

———o———

THE QUESTION ILLUSTRATED BY EXPERIENCE.

GRACE.

[*Sings.*

Hither, Sleep! A mother wants thee!
  Come with velvet arms!
Fold the baby that she grants thee
  To thy own soft charms!

Bear him into Dreamland lightly!
  Give him sight of flowers!

Do not bring him back till brightly
  Break the morning hours!

Close his eyes with gentle fingers!
  Cross his hands of snow!
Tell the angels where he lingers
  They must whisper low!

I will guard thy spell unbroken
  If thou hear my call;
Come then, Sleep! I wait the token
  Of thy downy thrall.

Now I see his sweet lips moving;
  He is in thy keep;
Other milk the babe is proving
  At the breast of sleep!

MARY.

Sleep, babe, the honeyed sleep of innocence!
Sleep like a bud; for soon the sun of life

With ardors quick and passionate shall rise,
And, with hot kisses, part the fragrant lips—
The folded petals of thy soul! Alas!
What feverish winds shall tease and toss thee, then!
What pride and pain, ambition and despair,
Desire, satiety, and all that fill
With misery life's fretful enterprise,
Shall wrench and blanch thee, till thou fall at last,
Joy after joy down fluttering to the earth,
To be apportioned to the elements!
I marvel, baby, whether it were ill
That he who planted thee should pluck thee now,
And save thee from the blight that comes on all.
I marvel whether it would not be well
That the frail bud should burst in Paradise,
On the full throbbing of an angel's heart!

GRACE

Oh, speak not thus! The thought is terrible.
He is my all; and yet, it sickens me

To think that he will grow to be a man.
If he were not a boy!

MARY.

Were not a boy?
That wakens other thoughts. Thank God for that!
To be a man, if aught, is privilege
Precious and peerless. While I bide content
The modest lot of woman, all my soul
Gives truest manhood humblest reverence.
It is a great and god-like thing to do!
'Tis a great thing, I think, to be a man.
Man fells the forests, ploughs and tills the fields,
And heaps the granaries that feed the world.
At his behest swift Commerce spreads her wings,
And tires the sinewy sea-birds as she flies,
Fanning the solitudes from clime to clime.
Smoke-crested cities rise beneath his hand,
And roar through ages with the din of trade.
Steam is the fleet-winged herald of his will,

Joining the angel of the Apocalypse
'Mid sound and smoke and wond'rous circumstance,
And with one foot upon the conquered sea
And one upon the subject land, proclaims
That space shall be no more. The lightnings veil
Their fiery forms to wait upon his thought,
And give it wing, as unseen spirits pause
To bear to God the burden of his prayer.
God crowns him with the gift of eloquence,
And puts a harp into his tuneful hands,
And makes him both his prophet and his priest.
'Twas in his form the great Immanuel
Revealed himself; the Apostolic Twelve,
Like those who since have ministered the Word,
Were men. 'Tis a great thing to be a man.

GRACE.

And fortunate to have an advocate
Across whose memory convenient clouds
Come floating at convenient intervals.

The harvest fields that man has honored most
Are those where human life is reaped like grain.
There never rose a mart, nor shone a sail,
Nor sprang a great invention into birth,
By other motive than man's love of gold.
It is for wrong that he is eloquent;
For lust that he indites his sweetest songs.
Christ was betrayed by treason of a man,
And scourged and hung upon a tree by men;
And the sad women who were at his cross,
And sought him early at the sepulchre,
And since that day, in gentle multitudes
Have loved and followed him, have been man's slaves,—
The victims of his power and his desire.

MARY.

And you, a wedded wife—well wedded, too,
Can say all this, and say it bitterly!

GRACE.

Perhaps because a wife; perhaps because—

MARY.

Hush, Grace! No more! I beg you, say no more.
Nay! I will leave you at another word;
For I could listen to a blasphemy,
Falling from bestial lips, with lighter chill
Than to the mad complainings of a soul
Which God has favored as he favors few.
I dare not listen when a woman's voice,
Which blessings strive to smother, flings them off
In mad contempt. I dare not hear the words
Whose utterance all the gentle loves dissuade
By kisses which are reasons, while a throng
Of friendships, comforts, and sweet charities—
The almoners of the All-Bountiful—
With folded wings stand sadly looking on.
Believe me, Grace, the pioneer of judgment—

Ordained, commissioned—is Ingratitude ;
For where it moves, good withers ; blessings die ;
Till a clean path is left for Providence,
Who never sows a good the second time
Till the torn bosom of the graceless soil
Is ready for the seed.

GRACE.

Oh, could you know
The anguish of my heart, you would not chide!
If I repine, it is because my lot
Is not the blessed thing it seems to you.
O Mary! Could you know! Could you but know!

MARY.

Then why not tell me all? You know me, love,
And know that secrets make their graves with me
So, tell me all ; for I do promise you
Such sympathy as God through suffering

Has given me power to grant to such as you.
I bought it dearly, and its largess waits
The opening of your heart.

GRACE.

I am ashamed,—
In truth, I am ashamed—to tell you all.
You will not laugh at me ?

MARY.

I laugh at you ?

GRACE.

Forgive me, Mary, for my heart is weak ;
Distrustful of itself and all the world.
Ah, well ! To what strange issues leads our life !
It seems but yesterday that you were brought
To this old house, an orphaned little girl,
Whose large shy eyes, pale cheeks, and shrinking ways

Filled all our hearts with wonder, as we stood
And stared at you, until your heart o'erfilled
With the oppressive strangeness, and you wept.
Yes, I remember how I pitied you—
I who had never wept, nor even sighed,
Save on the bosom of my gentle mother;
For my quick heart caught all your history
When with a hurried step you sought the sun,
And pressed your eyes against the window-pane
That God's sweet light might dry them. Well I knew,
Though all untaught, that you were motherless.
And I remember how I followed you,—
Embraced and kissed you—kissed your tears away—
Tears that came faster, till they bathèd the lips
That would have sealed their flooded fountain-heads;
And then we wound our arms around each other,
And passed out—out under the pleasant sky,
And stood among the lilies at the door.

I gave no formal comfort; you, no thanks;

For tears had been your language, kisses mine,
And we were friends. We talked about our dolls,
And all the pretty playthings we possessed.
Then we revealed, with childish vanity,
Our little stores of knowledge. I was full
Of a sweet marvel when you pointed out
The yellow thighs of bees that, half asleep,
Plundered the secrets of the lily-bells,
And called the golden pigment honey-comb.
And your black eyes were opened very wide
When I related how, one sunny day,
I found a well, half-covered, down the lane,
That was so deep and clear that I could see
Straight through the world, into another sky!

MARY.

Do you remember how the Guinea hens
Set up a scream upon the garden wall,
That frightened me to running, when you screamed
With laughter quite as loud?

GRACE.

Aye, very well;
But better still the scene that followed all.
Oh, that has lingered in my memory
Like that divinest dream of Raphael—
The Dresden virgin prisoned in a print—
That watched with me in sickness through long weeks,
And from its frame upon the chamber-wall
Breathed constant benedictions, till I learned
To love the presence like a Roman saint.

My mother called us in; and at her knee,
Embracing still, we stood, and felt her smile
Shine on our up-turned faces like the light
Of the soft summer moon. And then she stooped;
And when she kissed us, I could see the tears
Brimming her eyes. O sweet experiment!
To try if love of Jesus and of me
Could make our kisses equal to her lips!
Then straight my prescient heart set up a song,

And fluttered in my bosom like a bird.
I knew a blessing was about to fall,
As robins know the coming of the rain,
And bruit the joyous secret, ere its steps
Are heard upon the mountain tops. I knew
You were to be my sister; and my heart
Was almost bursting with its love and pride.
I could not wait to hear the kindly words
Our mother spoke—her counsels and commands—
For you were mine—my sister! So I tore
Your clinging hand from hers with rude constraint,
And took you to my chamber, where I played
With you, in selfish sense of property,
The whole bright afternoon.

And here again,
Within this same old chamber we are met.
We told our secrets to each other then;
Thus let us tell them now; and you shall be
To my grief-burdened soul what you have said,
So many times that I have been to yours.

MARY.

Alas! I never meant to tell my tale
To other ear than God's; but you have claims
Upon my confidence,—claims just rehearsed,
And other claims which you have never known.

GRACE.

And other claims which I have never known!
You speak in riddles, love. I only know
You grew to womanhood, were beautiful,
Were loved and wooed, were married and were blest;—
That after passage of mysterious years
We heard sad stories of your misery,
And rumors of desertion; but your pen
Revealed no secrets of your altered life.
Enough for me that you are here to-night.
And have an ear for sorrow, and a heart
Which disappointment has inhabited.

My history you know. A twelvemonth since
This fearful, festive night, and in this house,
I gave my hand to one whom I believed
To be the noblest man God ever made;—
A man who seemed to my infatuate heart
Heaven's chosen genius, through whose tuneful soul
The choicest harmonies of life should flow,
Growing articulate upon his lips
In numbers to enchant a willing world.
I cannot tell you of the pride that filled
My bosom, as I marked his manly form,
And read his soul through his effulgent eyes,
And heard the wondrous music of his voice,
That swept the chords of feeling in all hearts
With such divine persuasion as might grow
Under the transit of an angel's hand.
And, then, to think that I, a farmer's child,
Should be the woman culled from all the world
To be that man's companion,—to abide
The nearest soul to such a soul—to sit

Close by the fountain of his peerless life—
The welling centre of his loving thoughts—
And drink, myself, the sweetest and the best,—
To lay my head upon his breast, and feel
That of all precious burdens it had borne
That was most precious—Oh ! my heart was wild
With the delirium of happiness—
But, Mary, you are weeping !

MARY.

Mark it not.
Your words wake memories which you may guess,
And thoughts which you may sometime know—not now

GRACE.

Well, we were married, as I said; and I
Was not unthankful utterly, I think;
Though, if the awful question had come then,
And stood before me with a brow severe
And steady finger, bidding me decide

Which of the two I loved the more, the God
Who gave my husband to me, or his gift,
I know I should have groaned, and shut my eyes.

We passed a honeymoon whose atmosphere,
Flooded with inspiration, and embraced
By a wide sky set full of starry thoughts,
And constellated visions of delight,
Still wraps me in my dreams—itself a dream.
The full moon waned at last, and in my sky,
With horn inverted, gave its sign of tears;
And then, when wasted to a skeleton,
It sank into a heaving sea of tears
That caught its tumult from my sighing soul.
My husband, who had spent whole months with me,
Till he was wedded to my every thought,
Left me through dreary hours,—nay, days,—alone!
He pleaded business—business day and night;
Leaving me with a formal kiss at morn,
And meeting me with strange reserve at eve;

And I could mark the sea of tenderness
Upon whose beach I had sat down for life,
Hoping to feel for ever, as at first,
The love-breeze from its billows, and to clasp
With open arms the silver surf that ran
To wreck itself upon my bosom, ebb,
Day after day receding, till the sand
Grew dry and hot, and the old hulls appeared
Of hopes sent out upon that faithless main
Since woman loved, and he she loved was false.
Night after night I sat the evening out,
And heard the clock tick on the mantel-tree
Till it grew irksome to me, and I grudged
The careless pleasures of the kitchen maids
Whose distant laughter shocked the lapsing hours.

MARY.

But did your husband never tell the cause
Of this neglect ?

GRACE.

Never an honest word.
He told me he was writing; and, at home,
Sat down with heart absorbed and absent look.
I was offended, and upbraided him.
I knew he had a secret, and that from
The centre of its closely coiling folds
A cunning serpent's head, with forked tongue,
Swayed with a double story—one for me,
And one for whom I knew not—whom he knew.
His words, which wandered first as carelessly
As the free footsteps of a boy, were trained
To the stern paces of a sentinel
Guarding a prison door, and never tripped
With a suggestion.

I despaired at last
Of winning what I sought by wiles and prayers;
So, through long nights of sleeplessness I lay,
And held my ear beside his silent lips—

An eager cup—ready to catch the gush
Of the pent waters, if a dream-swung rod
Should smite his bosom. It was all in vain.
And thus months passed away, and all the while
Another heart was beating under mine.
May Heaven forgive me! but I grieved the charms
The unborn thing was stealing, for I felt
That in my insufficiency of power
I had no charm to lose.

MARY.

And did he not,
In this most tender trial of your heart,
Turn in relenting?—give you sympathy?

GRACE.

No—yes! Perhaps he pitied me, and that
Indeed was very pitiful; for what
Has love to do with pity? When a wife
Has sunk so hopelessly in the regard

Of him she loves that he can pity her,—
Has sunk so low that she may only share
The tribute which a mute humanity
Bestows on those whom Providence has struck
With helpless poverty, or foul disease;
She may be pitied, both by earth and heaven,
Because he pities her. A pitied child
That begs its bread from door to door is blest;
A wife who begs for love and confidence,
And gets but alms from pity, is accurst.

Well, time passed on; and rumor came at last
To tell the story of my husband's shame
And my dishonor. He was seen at night,
Walking in lonely streets with one whose eyes
Were blacker than the night,—whose little hand
Was clinging to his arm. Both were absorbed
In the half-whispered converse of the time;
And both, as if accustomed to the path,
Turned down an alley, climbed a flight of steps,

Entered a door, and closed it after them—
A door of adamant 'twixt hope and me.
I had my secret; and I kept it, too.
I knew his haunt, and it was watched for me,
Till doubt and prayers for doubt,—pale flowers
I nourished with my tears—were crushed
By the relentless hand of Certainty.

Oh, Mary! Mary! Those were fearful days.
My wrongs and all their shameful history
Were opened to me daily, leaf by leaf,
Though he had only shown their title-page:
That page was his; the rest were in my heart.
I knew that he had left my home for her's;
I knew his nightly labor was to feed
Other than me;—that he was loaded down
With cares that were the price of sinful love.

MARY.

Grace, in your heart do you believe all this?

I fear—I know—you do your husband wrong.
He is not competent for treachery.
He is too good, too noble, to desert
The woman whom he only loves too well.
You love him not!

GRACE.

I love him not? Alas!
I am more angry with myself than him
That, spite his falsehood to his marriage vows,
And spite my hate, I love the traitor still.
I love him not? Why am I here to-night—
Here where my girlhood's withered hopes are strewn
Through every room for him to trample on—
But in my pride to show him to you all,
With the dear child that publishes a love
That blessed me once, e'en if it curse me now?
You know I do my husband wrong! You think,
Because he can talk smoothly, and befool
A simple ear with pious sophistries,

He must be e'en the saintly man he seems.
We heard him talk to-night; it was done well.
I saw the triumph of his argument,
And I was proud, though full of spite the while.
His stuff was meant for me; and, with intent,
For selfish purpose, or in irony,
He tossed me bitterness, and called it sweet.
My heart rebelled, and now you know the cause
Of my harsh words to him.

MARY.

'Tis very sad!
Oh very—very sad! Pray you go on!
Who is this woman?

GRACE.

I have never learned.
I only know she stole my husband's heart,
And made me very wretched. I suppose
That at the time my little babe was born,

She went away; for David was at home
For many days. That pain was bliss to me—
I need no argument to teach me that—
Which caused neglect of her, and gave offence.
Since then, he has not where to go from me;
And, loving well his child, he stays at home.

So he lugs round his secret, and I mine.
I call him, husband; and he calls me, wife;
And I, who once was like an April day,
That finds quick tears in every cloud, have steeled
My heart against my fate, and now am calm.
I will live on; and though these simple folk
Who call me sister understand me not,
It matters little. There is one who does;
And he shall have no liberty of love
By any word of mine. 'Tis woman's lot,
And man's most weak and wicked wantonness.
Mine is like other husbands, I suppose;
No worse—no better.

MARY.

Ask you sympathy
Of such as I? I cannot give it you,
For you have shut me from the privilege.

GRACE.

I asked it once; you gave me unbelief.
I had no choice but to grow hard again.
'Tis my misfortune and my misery
That every hand whose friendly ministry
My poor heart craves, is held—withheld—by him;
And I must freeze that I may stand alone.

MARY.

And so, because one man is false, or you
Imagine him to be, all men are false;
Do I speak rightly?

GRACE.

Have it your own way.
Men fit to love, and fitted to be loved,

Are prone to falsehood. I will not gainsay
The common virtue of the common herd.
I prize it as I do the goodish men
Who hold the goodish stuff, and know it not.
These serve to fill an easy-going world,
And that to clothe it with complacency.

MARY.

I had not thought misanthropy like this
Could lodge with you; so I must e'en confess
A tale which never passed my lips before,
Nor sent its flush to any cheek but mine.
In this, I'll prove my friendship, if I lose
The friendship which demands the sacrifice.

I have come back, a worse than widowed wife;
Yet I went out with dream as bright as yours,—
Nay, brighter,—for the birds were singing then,
And apple-blossoms drifted on the ground
Where snow-flakes fell and flew when you were wed.

The skies were soft; the roses budded full;
The meads and swelling uplands fresh and green;—
The very atmosphere was full of love.
It was no girlish carelessness of heart
That kept my eyes from tears, as I went forth
From this dear shelter of the orphan child.
I felt that God was smiling on my lot,
And made the airs his angels to convey
To every sense and sensibility
The message of his favor. Every sound
Was music to me; every sight was peace;
And breathing was the drinking of perfume.
I said, content, and full of gratitude,
"This is as God would have it; and he speaks
These pleasant languages to tell me so."

But I had no such honey-moon as yours.
A few brief days of happiness, and then
The dream was over. I had married one
Who was the sport of vagrant impulses

We had not been a fortnight wed, when he
Came home to me with brandy in his brain—
A maudlin fool—for love like mine to hide
As if he were an unclean beast. O Grace!
I cannot paint the horrors of that night.
My heart, till then serene, and safely kept
In Trust's strong citadel, quaked all night long,
As tower and bastion fell before the rush
Of fierce convictions; and the tumbling walls
Boomed with dull throbs of ruin through my brain.
And there were palaces that leaned on this—
Castles of air, in long and glittering lines,
Which melted into air, and pierced the blue
That marks the star-strewn vault of heaven;—all fell,
With a faint crash like that which scares the soul
When dissolution shivers through a dream
Smitten by nightmare,—fell and faded all
To utter nothingness; and when the morn
Flamed up the East, and with its crimson wings
Brushed out the paling stars that all the night

In silent, slow procession, one by one,
Had gazed upon me through the open sash,
And passed along, it found me desolate.

The stupid dreamer at my side awoke,
And with such helpless anguish as they feel
Who know that they are weak as well as vile.
I saw, through all his forward promises,
Excuses, prayers, and pledges that were oaths
(What he, poor boaster, thought I could not see),
That he was shorn of will, and that his heart
Was as defenceless as a little child's;—
That underneath his fair good fellowship
He was debauched, and dead in love with sin;—
That love of me had made him what I loved,—
That I could only hold him till the wave
Of some o'erwhelming impulse should sweep in,
To lift his feet and bear him from my arms.
I felt that morn, when he went trembling forth,
With bloodshot eyes and forehead hot with woe,

That thenceforth strife would be 'twixt Hell and me—
The odds against me—for my husband's soul.

GRACE.

Poor dove! Poor Mary! Have you suffered thus?
You had not even pride to keep you up.
Were he my husband, I had left him then—
The ingrate!

MARY.

Not if you had loved as I;
Yet what you know is but a bitter drop
Of the full cup of gall that I have drained.
Had he left me unstained,—had I rebelled
Against the influence by which he sought
To bring me to a compromise with him,—
To make my shrinking soul meet his half way,—
It had been better; but he had an art,
When appetite or passion moved in him,
That clothed his sins with fair apologies,

And smoothed the wrinkles of a haggard guilt
With the good-natured hand of charity.
He knew he was a fool, he said, and said again;
But human nature would be what it was,
And life had never zest enough to bear
Too much dilution; those who work like slaves
Must have their days of frolic and of fun.
He doubted whether God would punish sin;
God was, in fact, too good to punish sin;
For sin itself was a compounded thing,
With weakness for its prime ingredient.
And thus he fooled a heart that loved him well;
And it went toward his heart by slow degrees,
Till Virtue seemed a frigid anchorite,
And Vice, a jolly fellow—bad enough,
But not so bad as Christian people think.

This was the cunning work of months—nay, years;
And, meantime, Edward sank from bad to worse.
But he had conquered. Wine was on his board,

Without my protest—with a glass for me!
His boon companions came and went, and made
My home their rendezvous with my consent.
The doughty oath that shocked my ears at first,
The doubtful jest that meant, or might not mean,
That which should set a woman's brow aflame,
Became at last (oh, shame of womanhood!)
A thing to frown at with a covert smile;
A thing to smile at with a decent frown;
A thing to steal a grace from, as I feigned
The innocence of deaf unconsciousness.
And I became a jester. I could jest
In a wild way on sacred things and themes;
And I have thought that in his better moods
My husband shrank with horror from the work
Which he had wrought in me.

I do not know
If, during all these downward-tending years,
Edward kept well his faith with me. I know

He used to tell me, in his boastful way,
How he had broke the hearts of pretty maids,
And that if he were single—well-a-day!
The time was past for thinking upon that!
And I had heart to toss the badinage
Back in his teeth, with pay of kindred coin;
And tell him lies to stir his bestial mirth;
And make my boast of conquests; and pretend
That the true heart I had bestowed on him
Had flown, and left him but an empty hand.

I had some days of pain and penitence.
I saw where all must end. I saw, too well,
Edward was growing idle,—that his form
Was gathering disgustful corpulence,—
That he was going down, and dragging me
To shame and ruin, beggary and death.
But judgment came, and overshadowed us;
And one quick bolt shot from the awful cloud
Severed the tie that bound two worthless lives.

What God hath joined together, God may part:—
Grace, have you thought of that?

GRACE.

You scare me, Mary!
Nay! Do not turn on me with such a look!
Its dread suggestion gives my heart a pang
That stops its painful beating.

MARY.

Let it pass!
One morn we woke with the first flush of light,
Our windows jarring with the cannonade
That ushered in the nation's festal day.
The village streets were full of men and boys,
And resonant with rattling mimicry
Of the black-throated monsters on the hill,—
A crashing, crepitating war of fire,—
And as we listened to the fitful feud,
Dull detonations came from far away,

Pulsing along the fretted atmosphere,
To tell that in the ruder villages
The day had noisy greeting, as in ours.

I know not why it was, but then, and there,
I felt a sinking sadness, passing tears—
A dark foreboding I could not dissolve,
Nor drive away. But when, next morn, I woke
In the sweet stillness of the Sabbath day,
And found myself alone, I knew that hearts
Which once have been God's temple, and in which
Something divine still lingers, feel the throb
Along the lines that bind them to The Throne
When judgment issues; and, though dumb and blind,
Shudder and faint with prophecies of ill.
How—by what cause—calamity should come,
I could not guess; that it was imminent,
Seemed just as certain as the morning's dawn.

We were to have a gala day, indeed.

There were to be processions and parades
A great oration in a mammoth tent,
With dinner following, and toast and speech
By all the wordy magnates of the town;
A grand balloon ascension afterwards;
And, in the evening, fireworks on the hill.
I knew that drink would flow from morn till night
In a wild maelstrom, circling slow around
The village rim, in bright careering waves,
But growing turbulent, and changed to ink
Around the village centre, till, at last,
The whirling, gurgling vortex would engulf
A maddened multitude in drunkenness.
And this was in my thought (the while my heart
Was palpitating with its nameless fear),
As, wrapped in vaguest dreams, and purposeless,
I laced my shoe and gazed upon the sky.
Then strange determination stirred in me;
And, turning sharply on my chair, I said,
"Edward, where'er you go to-day, I go!"

If I had smitten him upon the face,
It had not tingled with a hotter flame.
He turned upon me with a look of hate—
A something worse than anger—and, with oaths,
Raved like a fiend, and cursed me for a fool.
But I was firm; he could not shake my will;
So, through the morning, until afternoon,
He stayed at home, and drank and drank again,
Watching the clock, and pacing up and down,
Until, at length, he came and sat by me,
To try his hackneyed tricks of blandishment.
He had not meant, he said, to give offence;
But women in a crowd were out of place.
He wished to see the aeronauts embark,
And meet some friends; but there would be a throng
Of boys and drunken boors around the car,
And I should not enjoy it; more than this,
The rise would be a finer spectacle
At home than on the ground. I gave assent,
And he went out. Of course, I followed him;

For I had learned to read him, and I knew
There was some precious scheme of sin on foot.

The crowd was heavy, and his form was lost
Quick as it touched the mass; but I pressed on,
Wild shouts and laughter punishing my ears,
Till I could see the bloated, breathing cone,
As if it were some monster of the sky
Caught by a net and fastened to the earth—
A butt for jeers to all the merry mob.
But I was distant still; and if a man
In mad impatience tore a passage from
The crowd that pressed upon him, or a girl,
Frightened or fainting, was allowed escape,
I slid like water to the vacant space,
And thus, by deftly won advances, gained
The stand I coveted.

We waited long;
And as the curious gazers stood and talked

About the diverse currents of the air,
And wondered where the daring voyagers
Would find a landing-place, a young man said,
In words intended for a spicy jest,
A man and woman living in the town
Had taken passage overland for hell!

Then at a distance rose a scattering shout
That fixed the vision of the multitude,
Standing on eager tiptoe, and afar
I saw the crowd give way, and make a path
For the pale heroes of the crazy hour.
Hats were tossed wildly as they struggled on,
And the gap closed behind them, till, at length,
They stood within the ring. Oh, damning sight!
The woman was a painted courtezan;
The man, my husband! I was dumb as death.
My teeth were clenched together like a vice,
And every heavy heart-throb was a chill.
But there I stood, and saw the shame go on.

They took their seats; the signal gun was fired;
The cords were loosed; and then the billowy bulk
Shot toward the zenith!

Never bent the sky
With a more cloudless depth of blue than then;
And, as they rose, I saw his faithless arm
Slide o'er her shoulder, and her dizzy head
Drop on his breast. Then I became insane.
I felt that I was struggling with a dream—
A horrid phantasm I could not shake off.
The hollow sky was swinging like a bell;
The silken monster swinging like its tongue;
And as it reeled from side to side, the roar
Of voices round me rang, and rang again,
Tolling the dreadful knell of my despair.

At the last moment I could trace his form,
Edward leaned over from his giddy seat,
And tossed out something on the air. I saw

The little missive fluttering slowly down,
And stretched my hand to catch it, for I knew,
Or thought I knew, that it would come to me.
And it did come to me—as if it slid
Upon the cord that bound my heart to his—
Strained to its utmost tension—snapped at last.
I marked it as it fell. It was a rose.
I grasped it madly as it struck my hand,
And buried all its thorns within my palm;
But the fierce pain released my prisoned voice,
And, with a shriek, I staggered, swooned, and fell.

That night was brushed from life. A passing friend
Directed those who bore me rudely off;
And I was carried to my home, and laid
Entranced upon my bed. The Sabbath morn
That followed all this din and devilry
Swung noiseless wide its doors of yellow light,
And in the hallowed stillness I awoke.
My heart was still; I could not stir a hand.

I thought that I was dying, or was dead,—
That I had slipped through smooth unconsciousness
Into the everlasting silences.
I could not speak; but winning strength, at last,
I turned my eyes to seek for Edward's face,
And saw an unpressed pillow. He was gone!

I was oppressed with awful sense of loss;
And, as a mother, by a turbid sea
That has engulfed her fairest child, sits down
And moans over the waters, and looks out
With curious despair upon the waves,
Until she marks a lock of floating hair,
And by its threads of gold draws slowly in,
And clasps and presses to her frenzied breast
The form it has no power to warm again,
So I, beside the sea of memory,
Lay feebly moaning, yearning for a clew
By which to reach my own extinguished life.
It came. A burning pain shot through my palm,

And thorns awoke what thorns had put to sleep.
It all came back to me—the roar, the rush,
The upturned faces, the insane hurras,
The skyward shooting spectacle, the shame—
And then I swooned again.

GRACE.

But was he killed?
Did his foolhardy venture end in wreck?
Or did it end in something worse than wreck?
Surely, he came again!

MARY.

To me, no more.
He had his reasons, and I knew them soon;
But, first, the fire enkindled in my brain
Burnt through long weeks of fever—burnt my frame—
Until it lay upon the sheet as white
As the pale ashes of a wasted coal.
Then, when streng h came to me, and I could sit,

Braced by the double pillows that were mine,
A kind friend took my hand, and told me all.

The day that Edward left me was the last
He could have been my husband; for the next
Disclosed his infamy and my disgrace.
He was a thief, and had been one, for years,—
Defrauding those whose gold he held in trust;
And he was ruined—ruined utterly.
The very bed I sat on was not his,
Nor mine, except by tender charity.
A guilty secret menacing behind,
A guilty passion burning in his heart,
And, by his side, a guilty paramour,
He seized upon this reckless whim, and fled
From those he knew would curse him ere he slept.

My cup was filled with wormwood; and it grew
Bitter and still more bitter, day by day,
Changing from shame and hate, to stern revenge.

Life had no more for me. My home was lost;
My heart unfitted to return to this;
And, reckless of the future, I went forth—
A woman stricken, maddened, desperate.
I sought the city with as sure a scent
As vultures track a carcass through the air.
I knew him there, delivered up to sin,
And longed to taunt him with his infamy,—
To haunt his haunts; to sting his perjured soul
With sharp reproaches; and to scare his eyes
With visions of his work upon my face.

But God had other means than my revenge
To humble him, and other thought for me.
I saw him only once; we did not meet;
There was a street between us; yet it seemed
Wide as the unbridged gulf that yawns between
The rich man and the beggar.

'Twas at dawn.

I had arisen from the sleepless bed
Which my scant means had purchased, and gone forth
To taste the air, and cool my burning brow.
I wandered on, not knowing where I went,
Nor caring whither. There were few astir;
The market wagons lumbered slowly in,
Piled high with carcasses of slaughtered lambs,
Baskets of unhusked corn, and mint, and all
The fresh, green things that grow in country fields.
I read the signs—the long and curious names—
And wondered who invented them, and if
Their owners knew how very strange they were.
A corps of weary firemen met me once,
Late home from service, with their gaudy car,
And loud with careless curses. Then I stopped,
And chatted with a frowsy-headed girl
Who knelt among her draggled skirts, and scrubbed
The heel-worn door-steps of a faded house.
Then, as I left her, and resumed my walk,
I turned my eyes across the street, and saw

A sight which stopped my feet, my breath, my heart
It was my husband. Oh, how sadly changed!
His bloodshot eyes stared from an anxious face;
His hat was battered, and his clothes were torn
And splashed with mud. His poisoned frame
Had shrunk away, until his garments hung
In folds about him. Then I knew it all:
His life had been a measureless debauch
Since his most shameless flight; and in his eye,
Eager and strained, and peering down the stairs
That tumbled to the ante-rooms of hell,
I saw the thirst which only death can quench.
He did not raise his eyes; I did not speak;
There was no work for me to do on him;
And when, at last, he tottered down the steps
Of a dark gin-shop, I was satisfied,
And half relentingly retraced my way.

I cannot tell the story of the months
That followed this. I toiled and toiled for bread,

And for the shelter of one stingy room.
Temptation, which the hand of poverty
Bears oft seductively to woman's lips,
To me came not. I hated men like beasts;
Their flattering words, and wicked, wanton leers,
Sickened me with ineffable disgust.

At length there came a change. One warm Spring eve,
As I sat idly dreaming of the past,
And questioning the future, my quick ear
Caught sound of feet upon the creaking stairs,
And a light rap delivered at my door.
I said, "Come in!" with half defiant voice,
Although I longed to see a human face,
And needed labor for my idle hands.
But when the door was opened, and there stood
A man before me, with an eye as pure
And brow as fair as any little child's,
Matched with a form and carriage which combined
All manly beauty, dignity, and grace,

A quick blush overwhelmed my pallid cheeks,
And, ere I knew, and by no act of will,
I rose and gave him gentle courtesy.

He took a seat, and spoke with pleasant voice
Of many pleasant things—the pleasant sky,
The stars, the opening foliage in the park;
And then he came to business. He would have
A piece of exquisite embroidery;
My hand was cunning if report were true;
Would it oblige him? It would do, I said,
That which it could to satisfy his wish;
And when he took the delicate pattern out,
And spread the dainty fabric on his knees,
I knew he had a wife.

He went away
With kind "Good night," and said that, with my leave,
He'd call and watch the progress of the work.
I marked his careful steps adown the stairs,

And then, his brisk, firm tread upon the pave,
Till in the dull roar of the distant streets
It mingled and was lost. Then I was lost,—
Lost in a wild, wide-ranging reverie—
From which I roused not till the midnight hush
Was broken by the toll from twenty towers.

This is a man, I said; a man in truth;
My room has known the presence of a man,
And it has gathered dignity from him.
I felt my being flooded with new life.
My heart was warm; my poor, sore-footed thoughts
Sprang up full fledged through ether; and I felt
Like the sick woman who had touched the hem
Of Jesus' garment, when through all her veins
Leaped the swift tides of youth.

He had a wife!
Why, to a wrecked, forsaken thing like me
Did that thought bring a pang? I did not know;

But, truth to tell, it gave me stinging pain.
If he was noble, he was naught to me;
If he was great, it only made me less;
If he loved truly, I was not enriched.
So, in my selfishness, I almost cursed
The unknown woman, thought for whom had brought
Her loving husband to me. What was I
To him? Naught but a poor unfortunate,
Picking her bread up at a needle's point.
He'll come and criticise my handiwork,
I said, and when it is at last complete,
He'll draw his purse and give me so much gold;
And then, forgetting me for ever, go
And gather fragrant kisses for the boon,
From lips that do not know their privilege.
I could be nothing but the medium
Through which his love should pass to reach its shrine;
The glass through which the sun's electric beams
Kindles the rose's heart, and still remains
Chill and serene itself—without reward!

Then came to me the thought of my great wrong.
A man had spoiled my heart, degraded me;
A wanton woman had defrauded me;
I would get reparation how I could!
He must be something to me—I to him!
All men, however good, are weak, I thought;
And if I can arrest no beam of love
By right of nature or by leave of law,
I'll stain the glass! And the last words I said,
As I lay down upon my bed to dream,
Were those four words of sin: "I'll stain the glass"

GRACE.

Mary, I cannot hear you more; your tale,
So bitter and so passing pitiful
I have forgotten tears, and feel my eyes
Burn dry and hot with looking at your face,
Now gathers blackness, and grows horrible.

MARY.

Nay, you must hear me out; I cannot pause;
And have no worse to say than I have said—
Thank God, and him who put away my toils!

He came, and came again; and every charm
God had bestowed on me, or art could frame,
I used with keenest ingenuities
To fascinate the sensuous element
O'er which, mistrusted, and but half asleep,
His conscience and propriety stood guard.
I told with tears the story of my woe;
He listened to me with a thoughtful face,
And sadly sighed; and thus I won his ruth.
And then I told him how my life was lost;—
How earth had nothing more for me but pain;
Not e'en a friend. At this, he took my hand,
And said, out of his nobleness of heart,
That I should have an honest friend in him;
On which I bowed my head upon his arm,

And wept again, as if my heart would break
With the full pressure of its gratitude.
He put me gently off, and read my face:
I stood before him hopeless, helpless, his!
His swift soul gathered what I meant it should.
He sighed and trembled; then he crossed the floor,
And gazed with eye abstracted on the sky;
Then came and looked at me; then turned,
As if affrighted at his springing thoughts,
And, with abruptest movement, left the room.

This time he took with him the broidered thing
That I had wrought for him; and when I oped
The little purse that he rewarded me,
I found full golden payment five times told.
Given from pity? thought I,—that alone?
Is manly pity so munificent?
Pity has mixtures that it knows not of!

It was a cruel triumph, and I speak

Of it with utter penitence and shame.
I knew that he would come again ; I knew
His feet would bring him, though his soul rebelled
I knew that cheated heart of his would toy
With the seductive chains that gave it thrall,
And strive to reconcile its perjury
With its own conscience of the better way,
By fabrication of apologies
It knew were false.

And he did come again;
Confessing a strange interest in me,
And doing for me many kindly deeds.
I knew the nature of the sympathy
That drew him to my side, better than he ;
Though I could see that solemn change in him
Which every face will wear, when Heaven and Hell
Are struggling in the heart for mastery.
He was unhappy ; every sudden sound
Startled his apprehensions ; from his heart

Rose heavy suspirations, charged with prayer,
Desire, and deprecation, and remorse;—
Sighs like volcanic breathings—sighs that scorched
His parching lips and spread his face with ashes,—
Sighs born in such convulsions of the soul
That his strong frame quaked like Vesuvius,
Burdened with restless lava.

Day by day
I marked this dalliance with sinful thought,
Without a throb of pity in my heart.
I took his gifts, which brought immunity
From toil and care, as if they were my right.
Day after day I saw my power increase,
Until that noble spirit was a slave—
A craven, helpless, self-suspected slave.

But this was not to last—thank God and him!
One night he came, and there had been a change.
My hand was kindly taken, but not held

In the way wonted. He was self-possessed;
The powers of darkness and his Christian heart
Had had a struggle—his the victory;
And on his manly brow the benison
Of a majestic peace had been imposed.
Was I to lose the guerdon of my guile?
He was my all, and by the only means
Left to a helpless, reckless thing, like me:
My heart made pledge the strife should be renewed.
I took no notice of his altered mood,
But strove, by all the tricks of tenderness,
To fan to life again the drooping flame
Within his heart;—with what success, at last,
The sequel shall reveal.

Strange fire came down
Responsive to my call, and the quick flash
That shrivelled resolution, vanquished will,
And with a blood-red flame consumed the crown
Of peace upon his brow, taught him how weak—

How miserably imbecile—he had become,
Tampering with temptation. Such a groan,
Wrung from such agony, as then he breathed,
Pray Heaven my ears may never hear again!
He smote his forehead with his rigid palm,
And sank, as if the blow had stunned him, to his
knees,
And there, with face pressed hard upon his hands
Gave utterance to frenzied sobs and prayers—
The wild articulations of despair.
I was confounded. He—a man—thought I,
Blind with remorse by simple look at sin!
And I—a woman—in the devil's hands,
Luring him Hellward with no blush of shame!
The thought came swift from God, and pierced my
heart,
Like a barbed arrow; and it quivered there
Through whiles of tumult—quivered—and was fast.

Thus, while I stood and marked his kneeling form,

Still shocked by deep convulsions, such a light
Illumed my soul, and flooded all the room,
That, without thought, I said, "The Lord is here!"
Then straight my spirit heard these wondrous words:
"Tempted in all points like ourselves, was He—
Tempted, but sinless." Oh, what majesty
Of meaning did those precious words convey!
'Twas through temptation, thought I, that the Lord—
The mediator between God and men—
Reached down the hand of sympathetic love
To meet the grasp of lost Humanity;
And this man, kneeling, has the Lord in him,
And comes to mediate 'twixt Christ and me,
"Tempted but sinless;"—one hand grasping mine,
The other Christ's.

Why had he suffered thus?
Why had his heart been led far down to mine,
To beat in sinful sympathy with mine,
But that my heart should cling to his and him,

And follow his withdrawal to the heights
From whence he had descended? Then I learned
Why Christ was tempted; and, as broad and full,
The heart of the great secret was revealed,
And I perceived God's dealings with my soul,
I knelt beside the tortured man and wept,
And cried to Heaven for mercy. As I prayed,
My soul cast off its shameful enterprise;
And when it fell, I saw my godless self—
My own degraded, tainted, guilty heart,
Which it had hidden from me. Oh, the pang—
The poignant throe of uttermost despair—
That followed the discovery! I felt
That I was lost beyond the grace of God;
And my heart turned with instinct sure and swift
To the strong struggler, praying at my side,
And begged his succor and his prayers. I felt
That he must lead me up to where the hand
Of Jesus could lay hold on me, or I was doomed.

Temptation's spell was past. He took my hand,
And, as he prayed that we might be forgiven,
And pledged our future loyalty to God
And his white throne within our hearts, I gave
Responses to each promise; then I crowned
His closing utterance with such Amen
As weak hearts, conscious of their weakness, give
When, bowed to dust, and clinging to the robes
Of outraged mercy, they devote themselves
Once and for ever to the pitying Christ.

Then we arose and stood upon our feet.
He gave me no reproaches, but with voice
Attempered to his altered mood, confessed
His own blameworthiness, and pressed the prayer
That I would pardon him, as he believed
That God had pardoned; but my heart was full,—
So full of its sore sense of wrong to him,
Of the deep guilt of shameful purposes
And treachery to worthy womanhood,

That I could not repeat his Christian words,
Asking forbearance on my own behalf.

He sat before me for a golden hour;
And gave me counsel and encouragement,
Till, like broad gates, the possibilities
Of a serener and a higher life
Were thrown wide open to my eager feet,
And I resolved that I would enter in,
And, with God's gracious help, go no more out.

For weeks he watched me with stern carefulness,
Nourished my resolution, prayed with me,
And led me, step by step, to higher ground,
Till, gathering impulse in the upward walk,
And strength in purer air, and keener sight
In the sweet light that dawned upon my soul,
I grasped the arm of Jesus, and was safe.
And now, when I look back upon my life,
It seems as if that noble man were sent

To give me rescue from the pit of death.
But from his distant height he could not reach
And act upon my soul; so Heaven allowed
Temptation's ladder 'twixt his soul and mine
That they might meet and yield his mission thrift.
I doubt not in my grateful soul to-night
That had he stayed within his higher world,
And tried to call me to him, I had spurned
Alike his mission and his ministry.
That he was tempted, was at once my sin
And my salvation. That he sinned in thought,
And fiercely wrestled with temptation, won
For his own spirit that humility
Which God had sought to clothe him with in vain,
By other measures, and that strength which springs
From a great conflict and a victory.
We talked of this; and on our bended knees
We blessed the Great Dispenser for the means
By which we both had learned our sinful selves,
And found the way to a diviner life.

So, with my chastened heart and life, I come
Back to my home, to live—perhaps to die.
God's love has been in all this discipline;
God's love has used those awful sins of mine
To make me good and happy. I can mourn
Over my husband; I can pray for him,
Nay, I forgive him; for I know the power
With which temptation comes to stronger men.
I know the power with which it came to me.

And now, dear Grace, my story is complete.
You have received it with dumb wonderment,
And it has been too long. Tell me what thought
Stirs in your face, and waits for utterance.

GRACE.

That I have suffered little—trusted less;
That I have failed in charity, and been
Unjust to all men—specially to one.
I did not think there lived a man on earth

Who had such virtue as this friend of yours,—
Weak, and yet strong. 'Twere but humanity
To give him pity in his awful strife;
To stint the meed of reverence and praise
For his triumphant conquest of himself,
Were infamy. I love and honor him;
And if I knew my husband were as strong,
I could fall down before, and worship him;
I could fall down, and wet his feet with tears—
Tears penitential for the grievous wrong
That I have done him. But alas! alas!
The thought comes back again. O God in Heaven!
Help me with patience to await the hour
When the great purpose of thy discipline
Shall be rev aled, and, like this chastened one,
I can behold it, and be satisfied.

MARY.

Hark! They are calling us below, I think.

We must go down. We'll talk of this again
When we have leisure. Kiss the little one,
And thank his weary brain it sleeps so well.

[*They descend.*

SECOND EPISODE.

———o———

LOCALITY—*The Kitchen.*

PRESENT—JOSEPH. SAMUEL, REBEKAH, *and other* CHILDREN.

———o———

THE QUESTION ILLUSTRATED BY STORY.

JOSEPH.

Have we not had "Button-Button" enough,
And "Forfeits," and all such silly stuff?

SAMUEL.

Well, we were playing "Blind-Man's-Buff"
Until you fell, and rose in a huff,

And declared the game was too rude and rough.
Poor boy! What a pity he isn't tough!

ALL.

Ha! ha! ha! what a pretty boy!
Papa's delight, and mamma's joy!
Wouldn't he like to go to bed,
And have a cabbage-leaf on his head?

JOSEPH.

Laugh, if you like to! Laugh till you're gray;
But I guess you'd laugh another way
If you'd hit your toe, and fallen like me,
And cut a bloody gash in your knee,
And bumped your nose and bruised your shin,
Tumbling over the rolling-pin
That rolled to the floor in the awful din
That followed the fall of the row of tin
That stood upon the dresser.

SAMUEL.

Guess again—dear little guesser!
You wouldn't catch this boy lopping his wing,
Or whining over anything.
So stir your stumps,
Forget your bumps,
Get out of your dumps,
And up and at it again;
For the clock is striking ten,
And Ruth will come pretty soon and say,
"Go to your beds
You sleepy heads!"
So—quick! What shall we play?

REBEKAH.

I wouldn't play any more,
For Joseph is tired and sore
With his fall upon the floor.

ALL.

Then he shall tell a story.

JOSEPH.

About old Mother Morey ?

ALL.

No ! Tell us another.

JOSEPH.

About my brother ?

REBEKAH.

Now, Joseph, you shall be good,
And do as you'd be done by;
We didn't mean to be rude
When you fell and began to cry;
We wanted to make you forget your pain;
But it frets you, and we'll not laugh again.

JOSEPH.

Well, if you'll all sit still,
And not be frisking about,
Nor utter a whisper till
You've heard my story out,
I'll tell you a tale as weird
As ever you heard in your lives,
Of a man with a long blue beard,
And the way he treated his wives.

ALL.

Oh, that will be nice!
We'll be still as mice.

JOSEPH.

[*Relates the old story of Blue Beard, and* DAVID *and* RUTH *enter from the cellar unperceived.*

Centuries since there flourished a man,
(A cruel old Tartar as rich as the Khan,)

Whose castle was built on a splendid plan,
  With gardens and groves and plantations;
But his shaggy beard was as blue as the sky,
And he lived alone, for his neighbors were shy,
And had heard hard stories, by the by,
  About his domestic relations.

Just on the opposite side of the plain
A widow abode, with her daughters twain;
And one of them—neither cross nor vain—
  Was a beautiful little treasure;
So he sent them an invitation to tea,
And having a natural wish to see
His wonderful castle and gardens, all three
  Said they'd do themselves the pleasure.

As soon as there happened a pleasant day,
They dressed themselves in a sumptuous way,
And rode to the castle as proud and gay
  As silks and jewels could make them;

And they were received in the finest style,
And saw everything that was worth their while,
In the halls of Blue Beard's grand old pile,
  Where he was so kind as to take them.

The ladies were all enchanted quite;
For they found old Blue Beard so polite
That they did not suffer at all from fright,
  And frequently called thereafter;
Then he offered to marry the younger one,
And as she was willing the thing was done,
And celebrated by all the ton
  With feasting and with laughter.

As kind a husband as ever was seen
Was Blue Beard then, for a month, I ween;
And she was as proud as any queen,
  And as happy as she could be, too;
But her husband called her to him one day,
And said, "My dear, I am going away;

It will not be long that I shall stay;
  There is business for me to see to.

"The keys of my castle I leave with you;
But if you value my love, be true,
And forbear to enter the Chamber of Blue!
  Farewell, Fatima! Remember!"
Fatima promised him; then she ran
To visit the rooms with her sister Ann;
But when she had finished the tour, she began
  To think about the Blue Chamber.

Well, the woman was curiously inclined,
So she left her sister and prudence behind,
(With a little excuse) and started to find
  The mystery forbidden.
She paused at the door;—all was still as night!
She opened it: then through the dim, blue light
There blistered her vision the horrible sight
  That was in that chamber hidden.

The room was gloomy and damp and wide,
And the floor was red with the bloody tide
From headless women, laid side by side,
  The wives of her lord and master!
Frightened and fainting, she dropped the key,
But seized it and lifted it quickly; then she
Hurried as swiftly as she could flee
  From the scene of the disaster.

She tried to forget the terrible dead,
But shrieked when she saw that the key was red,
And sickened and shook with an awful dread
  When she heard Blue Beard was coming.
He did not appear to notice her pain;
But he took his keys, and seeing the stain,
He stopped in the middle of the refrain
  That ho had been quietly humming.

"Mighty well, madam!" said he, "mighty well!
What does this little blood-stain tell?

You've broken your promise; prepare to dwell
  With the wives I've had before you!
You've broken your promise, and you shall die."
Then Fatima, supposing her death was nigh,
Fell on her knees and began to cry,
  "Have mercy, I implore you!"

"No!" shouted Blue Beard, drawing his sword;
"You shall die this very minute," he roared.
"Grant me time to prepare to meet my Lord,"
  The terrified woman entreated.
"Only ten minutes," he roared again;
And holding his watch by its great gold chain,
He marked on the dial the fatal ten,
  And retired till they were completed.

"Sister, oh, sister, fly up to the tower!
Look for release from this murderer's power!
Our brothers should be here this very hour,—
  Speak! Does there come assistance?

"No: I see nothing but sheep on the hill."
"Look again, sister!" "I'm looking still,
But naught can I see, whether good or ill,
Save a flurry of dust in the distance."

"Time's up!" shouted Blue Beard, out from his room;
"This moment shall witness your terrible doom,
And give you a dwelling within the room
Whose secrets you have invaded."
"Comes there no help for my terrible need?"
"There are horsemen twain riding hither with speed."
"Oh! tell them to ride very fast indeed,
Or I must meet death unaided."

"Time's fully up! Now have done with your prayer,"
Shouted Blue Beard, swinging his sword on the stair;
Then he entered, and grasping her beautiful hair,
Swung his glittering weapon around him;
But a loud knock rang at the castle gate,
And Fatima was saved from her horrible fate

For, shocked with surprise, he paused too late;
  And then the two soldiers found him.

They were her brothers, and quick as they knew
What the fiend was doing, their swords they drew,
And attacked him fiercely, and ran him through,
  So that soon he was mortally wounded.
With a wild remorse was his conscience filled
When he thought of the hapless wives he had killed;
But quickly the last of his blood was spilled,
  And his dying groan was sounded.

As soon as Fatima recovered from fright,
She embraced her brothers with great delight;
And they were as glad and as grateful quite
  As she was glad and grateful.
Then they all went out from that scene of pain,
And sought in quietude to regain
Their minds, which had come to be quite insane,
  In a place so horrid and hateful.

'Twas a private funeral Blue Beard had;
For the people knew he was very bad,
And, though they said nothing, they all were glad
  For the fall of the evil-doer;
But Fatima first ordered some graves to be made,
And there the unfortunate ladies were laid,
And after some painful months, with the aid
  Of her friends, her spirits came to her.

Then she cheered the hearts of the suffering poor,
And an acre of land around each door
And a cow and a couple of sheep, or more,
  To her tenantry she granted.
So all of them had enough to eat,
And their love for her was so complete
They would kiss the dust from her little feet,
  Or do anything she wanted.

SAMUEL.

Capital! Capital! Wasn't it good!

I should like to have been her brother;
If I had been one, you may guess there would
Have been little work for the other.
I'd have run him right through the heart, just so.
And cut off his head at a single blow,
And killed him so quickly he'd never know
What it was that struck him, wouldn't I, Joe?

JOSEPH.

You are very brave with your bragging tongue;
But if you had been there, you'd have sung
  A very different tune.
Poor Blue Beard! He would have been afraid
Of a little boy with a penknife blade,
  Or a tiny pewter spoon!

SAMUEL.

  It makes no difference what you say
  (Pretty little boy, afraid to play!)

But it served him rightly any way,
  And gave him just his due.
And wasn't it good that his little wife
Should live in his castle the rest of her life,
  And have all his money too?

REBEKAH.

I'm thinking of the ladies who
Were lying in the Chamber Blue,
With all their small necks cut in two.

I see them lying, half a score,
In a long row upon the floor,
Their cold, white bosoms marked with gore.

I know the sweet Fatima would
Have put their heads on if she could;
And made them live—she was so good;

And washed their faces at the sink;
But Blue Beard was not sane, I think:
I wonder if he did not drink!

For no man in his proper mind
Would be so cruelly inclined
As to kill ladies who were kind.

RUTH.

[*Stepping forward with* DAVID

Story and comment alike are bad;
These little fellows are raving mad
With thinking what they should do,
Supposing their sunny-eyed sister had
Given her heart—and her head—to a lad
Like the man with the Beard of Blue.
Each little jacket
Is now a packet
Of murderous thoughts and fancies;
Oh, the gentle trade
By which fiends are made

With the ready aid
Of these bloody old romances!
And the little girl takes the woman's turn,
And thinks that the old curmudgeon
Who owned a castle, and rolled in gold
Over fields and gardens manifold,
And kept in his house a family tomb,
With his bowling course and his billiard-room,
Where he could preserve his precious dead,
Who took the kiss of the bridal bed
From one who straightway took their head,
And threw it away with the pair of gloves
In which he wedded his hapless loves,
Had some excuse for his dudgeon.

DAVID.

We learn by contrast to admire
The beauty that enchains us;
And know the object of desire
By that which pains us.

The roses blushing at the door,
  The lapse of leafy June,
The singing birds, the sunny shore,
      The summer moon;—

All these entrance the eye or ear
  By innate grace and charm;
But o'er them, reaching through the year
      Hangs Winter's arm,

To give to memory the sign,
  The index of our bliss,
And show by contrast how divine
      The Summer is.

From chilling blasts and stormy skies,
  Bare hills and icy streams,
Touched into fairest life arise
      Our summer dreams.

And virtue never seems so fair
  As when we lift our gaze
From the red eyes and bloody hair
      That vice displays.

We are too low,—our eyes too dark
  Love's height to estimate,
Save as we note the sunken mark
      Of brutal Hate.

So this ensanguined tale shall move
  Aright each little dreamer,
And Blue Beard teach them how to love
      The sweet Fatima.

They hate his crimes, and it is well;
  They pity those who died;
Their sense of justice when he fell
      Was satisfied.

No fierce revenges are the fruit
Of their just indignation;
They sit in judgment on the brute,
And condemnation;

And turn to her, his rescued wife,
Her deeds so kind and human,
And love the beauty of her life,
And bless the woman.

RUTH.

That is the way I supposed you would twist it;
And now that the boys are disposed of,
And the moral so handsomely closed off,
What do you say of the girl? That she missed it,
When she thought of old Blue Beard as some do of Judas,
Who with this notion essay to delude us:
That when he relented,
And fiercely repented,

He was hardly so bad
As he commonly had
The fortune to be represented?

DAVID.

The noblest pity in the earth
Is that bestowed on sin.
The Great Salvation had its birth
That ruth within.

The girl is nearest God, in fact;
The boy gives crime its due;
She blames the author of the act,
And pities too.

Thus, from this strange excess of wrong,
Her tender heart has caught
The noblest truth, the sweetest song,
The Saviour taught.

So, more than measured homily,
  Of sage, or priest, or preacher,
Is this wild tale of cruelty
          Love's gentle teacher.

It tells of sin, its deep remorse,
  Its fitting recompense,
And vindicates the tardy course
          Of Providence.

These boyish bosoms are on fire
  With chivalric possession,
And burn with just and manly ire
          Against oppression.

The glory and the grace of life,
  And Love's surpassing sweetness,
Rise from the monster to the wife
          In high completeness;

And thence look down with mercy's eye
 On sin's accurst abuses,
And seek to wrest from charity
 Some fair excuses.

RUTH.

These greedy mouths are watering
For the fruit within the basket;
And, although they will not ask it,
Their jack-knives all are burning
And their eager hands are yearning
 For the peeling and the quartering.
So let us have done with our talk;
For they are too tired to say their prayers,
And the time is come they should walk
From the story below to the story up stairs.

THIRD MOVEMENT.

DRAMATIC.

THE THIRD MOVEMENT.

——o——

LOCALITY—*The Kitchen.*

PRESENT—David, Ruth, John, Peter, Prudence, *and* Patience.

——o——

THE QUESTION ILLUSTRATED BY THE DENOUEMENT

JOHN.

Since the old gentleman retired to bed,
Things have gone strangely. David, here, and Ruth,
Have wasted thirty minutes underground
In explorations. One would think the house
Covered the entrance of the Mammoth Cave,
And they had lost themselves. Mary and Grace

Still hold their chamber and their conference,
And pour into each other's greedy ears
Their stream of talk, whose low, monotonous hum,
Would lull to slumber any storm but this.
The children are play-tired and gone to bed;
And one may know by looking round the room
Their place of sport was here. And we, plain folk,
Who have no gift of speech, especially
On themes which we and none may understand,
Have yawned and nodded in the great square room,
And wondered if the parted family
Would ever meet again.

RUTH.

John, do you see
The apples and the cider on the hearth?
If I remember rightly, you discuss
Such themes as these with noticeable zest
And pleasant tokens of intelligence;

Rather preferring scanty company
To the full circle. So, sir, take the lead,
And help yourself.

JOHN.

Aye! That I will, and give
Your welcome invitation currency,
In the old-fashioned way. Come! Help yourselves!

DAVID.

[*Looking out from the window*

The ground is thick with sleet, and still it falls!
The atmosphere is plunging like the sea
Against the woods, and pouring on the night
The roar of breakers, while the blinding spray
O'erleaps the barrier, and comes drifting on
In lines as level as the window-bars.
What curious visions, in a night like this,
Will the eye conjure from the rocks and trees,
And zigzag fences! I was almost sure

I saw a man staggering along the road
A moment since; but instantly the shape
Dropped from my sight. Hark! Was not that a call—
A human voice? There's a conspiracy
Between my eyes and ears to play me tricks,
Else wanders there abroad some hapless soul
Who needs assistance. There he stands again,
And with unsteady essay strives to breast
The tempest. Hush! Did you not hear that cry?
Quick, brothers! We must out, and give our aid.
None but a dying and despairing man
Ever gave utterance to a cry like that.
Nay, wait for nothing. Follow me!

RUTH.

Alas!
Who can he be, who on a night like this,
And on this night, of all nights in the year,
Holds to the highway, homeless?

PRUDENCE.

Probably
Some neighbor, started from his home in quest
Of a physician; or, more likely still,
Some poor inebriate, sadly overcome
By his sad keeping of the holiday.
I hope they'll give him quarters in the barn;
If he sleep here, there'll be no sleep for me.

PATIENCE.

I'll not believe it was a man at all;
David and Ruth are always seeing things
That no one else sees.

RUTH.

I see plainly now
What we shall all see plainly, soon enough.
The man is dead, and they are bearing him
As if he were a log. Quick! Stir the fire,

And clear the settle! We must lay him there.
I will bring cordials, and flannel stuffs
With which to chafe him; open wide the door.

[The men enter, bearing a body apparently lifeless, which they lay upon the settle.

DAVID.

Now do my bidding, orderly and swift;
And we may save from death a fellow man.
Peter, relieve him of those frozen shoes,
And wrap his feet in flannel. This way, Ruth!
Administer that cordial yourself.
John, you are strong, and that rough hand of yours
Will chafe him well. Work with a will, I say!

* * * * * * *

My hand is on his heart, and I can feel
Both warmth and motion. If we persevere,
He will be saved. Work with a will, I say!

* * * * * * *

A groan? Ha! That is good. Another groan?
Better and better!

RUTH.

It is down at last!—
A spoonful of the cordial. His breath
Comes feebly, but is warm upon my hand.

DAVID.

Give him brisk treatment, and persistent, too;
And we shall be rewarded presently,
For there is life in him.

*   *   *   *   *   *   *

He moves his lips
And tries to speak.

*   *   *   *   *   *   *

And now he opes his eyes.
What eyes! How wandering and wild they are!

[*To the stranger*

We are your friends. We found you overcome
By the cold storm without, and brought you in.
We are your friends, I say; so be at ease,

And let us do according to your need.
What is your wish?

STRANGER.

My friends? O God in Heaven!
They've cheated me! I'm in the hospital.
Oh, it was cruel to deceive me thus!
No, you are not my friends. What bitter pain
Racks my poor body!

DAVID.

Poor man, how he raves!
Let us be silent while the warmth and wine
Provoke his sluggish blood to steady flow,
And each dead sense comes back to life again,
O'er the same path of torture which it trod
When it went out from him. He'll slumber soon,
And, when he wakens, we may talk with him.

PRUDENCE

[*Sotto voce.*

Shall I not call the family? I think
Mary and Grace must both be very cold;
And they know nothing of this strange affair.
I'll wait them at the landing, and secure
Their silent entrance.

DAVID.

If it please you—well.

[PRUDENCE *retires, and returns with* GRACE *and* MARY

MARY.

Why! We heard nothing of it—Grace and I:—
What a cadaverous hand! How blue and thin!

DAVID.

At his first wild awaking he bemoaned
His fancied durance in a hospital;

And since he spoke so strangely, I have thought
He may have fled a mad-house. Matters not!
We've done our duty, and preserved his life.

MARY.

Shall I disturb him if I look at him?
I'm strangely curious to see his face.

DAVID.

Go. Move you carefully, and bring us word
Whether he sleeps.

[MARY *rises, goes to the settle, and sinks back fainting.*

Why! What ails the girl?
I thought her nerves were iron. Dash her brow
And bathe her temples!

MARY.

There—there,—that will do.
'Tis over now.

DAVID.

The man is speaking. Hush!

STRANGER.

Oh, what a heavenly dream! But it is past,
Like all my heavenly dreams, for never more
Shall dream entrance me. Death has never dreams,
But everlasting wakefulness. The eye
Of the quick spirit that has dropped the flesh
May close no more in slumber.

* * * * * * *

I must die!
This painless spell which binds my weary limbs—
This peace ineffable of soul and sense—
Is dissolution's herald, and gives note
That life is conquered and the struggle o'er.
But I had hoped to see her ere I died;
To kneel for pardon, and implore one kiss,
Pledge to my soul that in the coming heaven
We should not meet as strangers, but rejoin

Our hearts and lives so madly sundered here,
Through fault and freak of mine. But it is well
God's will be done!

* * * * * * *

I dreamed that I had reached
The old red farm-house,—that I saw the light
Flaming as brightly as in other times
It flushed the kitchen windows; and that forms
Were sliding to and fro in joyous life,
Restless to give me welcome. Then I dreamed
Of the dear woman who went out with me
One sweet spring morning, in her own sweet spring,
To——wretchedness and ruin. Oh, forgive—
Dear, pitying Christ, forgive this cruel wrong,
And let me die! Oh, let me—let me die!
Mary! my Mary! Could you only know
How I have suffered since I fled from you,—
How I have sorrowed through long months of pain,
And prayed for pardon,—you would pardon me.

DAVID.

[*Sotto voce.*

Mary, what means this? Does he dream alone,
Or are we dreaming?

MARY.

Edward, I am here!
I am your Mary! Know you not my face?
My husband, speak to me! Oh, speak once more!
This is no dream, but kind reality.

EDWARD.

[*Raising himself, and looking wildly around.*

You, Mary? Is this heaven, and am I dead?
I did not know you died: when did you die?
And John and Peter, Grace and little Ruth
Grown to a woman; are they all with you?
'Tis very strange! O pity me, my friends!
For God has pitied me, and pardoned, too

Else I should not be here. Nay, you seem cold,
And look on me with sad severity.
Have you no pardoning word—no smile for me?

MARY.

This is not Heaven's but Earth's reality;
This is the farm-house—these your wife and friends.
I hold your hand, and I forgive you all.
Pray you recline! You are not strong enough
To bear this yet.

EDWARD.

[*Sinking back.*

O toiling heart! O sick and sinking heart!
Give me one hour of service, ere I die!
This is no dream. This hand is precious flesh,
And I am here where I have prayed to be.
My God, I thank thee! Thou hast heard my prayer,
And, in its answer, given me a pledge
Of the acceptance of my penitence.

How have I yearned for this one priceless hour!
Cling to me, dearest, while my feet go down
Into the silent stream; nor loose your hold,
Till angels grasp me on the other side.

MARY.

Edward, you are not dying—must not die;
For only now are we prepared to live.
You must have quiet, and a night of rest.
Be silent, if you love me!

EDWARD.

If I love?
Ah, Mary! never till this blessed hour,
When power and passion, lust and pride are gone,
Have I perceived what wedded love may be;—
Unutterable fondness, soul for soul;
Profoundest tenderness between two hearts
Allied by nature, interlocked by life.

I know that I shall die; but the low clouds
That closed my mental vision have retired,
And left a sky as clear and calm as Heaven.
I must talk now, or never more on earth;
So do not hinder me.

MARY.

[*Weeping*

Have you a wish
That I can gratify? Have you any words
To send to other friends?

EDWARD.

I have no friends
But you and these, and only wish to leave
My worthless name and memory redeemed
Within your hearts to pitying respect.
I have no strength, and it becomes me not,
To tell the story of my life of sin.
I was a drunkard, thief, adulterer;

And fled from shame, with shame, to find remorse.
I had but few months of debauchery,
Pursued with mad intent to damp or drown
The flames of a consuming conscience, when
My body, poisoned, crippled with disease,
Refused the guilty service of my soul,
And at mid-day fell prone upon the street.
Thence I was carried to a hospital,
And there I woke to that delirium
Which none but drunkards this side of the pit
May even dream of.

But at last there came,
With abstinence and kindly medicines,
Release from pain and peaceful sanity;
And then Christ found me, ready for His hand.
I was not ready for Him when He came
And asked me for my youth; and when He knocked
At my heart's door in manhood's early prime
With tenderest monitions, I debarred

His waiting feet with promise and excuse;
And when, in after years, absorbed in sin,
The gentle summons swelled to thunderings
That echoed through the chambers of my soul
With threats of vengeance, I shut up my ears;
And then He went away, and let me rush
Without arrest, or protest, toward the pit.
I made swift passage downward, till, at length,
I had become a miserable wreck—
Pleasure behind me; only pain before;
My life lived out; the fires of passion dead;
Without a friend; no pride, no power, no hope;
No motive in me e'en to wish for life.
Then, as I said, Christ came, with stern and sad
Reminders of His mercy and my guilt,
And the door fell before Him.

I went out,
And trod the wildernesses of remorse
For many days. Then from their outer verge,

Tortured and blinded, I plunged madly down
Into the sullen bosom of despair;
But strength from Heaven was given me, and pre
served
Breath in my bosom, till a light streamed up
Upon the other shore, and I struck out
On the cold waters, struggling for my life.
Fainting I reached the beach, and on my knees
Climbed up the thorny hill of penitence,
Till I could see, upon its distant brow,
The Saviour beck'ning. Then I ran—I flew—
And grasped his outstretched hand. It lifted me
High on the everlasting rock, and then
It folded me, with all my griefs and tears,
My sin-sick body and my guilt-stained soul,
To the great heart that throbs for all the world.

MARY.

Dear Lord, I bless thee! Thou hast heard my prayer,

And saved the wanderer! Hear it once again,
And lengthen out the life thou hast redeemed!

EDWARD.

Mary, my wife, forbear! I may not give
Response to such petition. I have prayed
That I may die. When first the love Divine
Received me on its bosom, and in mine
I felt the springing of another life,
I begged the Lord to grant me two requests:
The first that I might die, and in that world
Where passion sleeps, and only influence
From Him and those who cluster at His throne
Breathes on the soul, the germ of His great life,
Bursting within me, might be perfected.
The second, that your life, my love, and mine
Might be once more united on the earth
In holy marriage, and that mine might be
Breathed out at last within your loving arms.

One prayer is granted, and the other waits
But a brief space for its accomplishment.

MARY.

But why this prayer to die? Still loving me,—
With the great motive for desiring life
And the deep secret of enjoyment won,—
Why pray for death?

EDWARD.

Do you not know me, Mary?
I am afraid to live, for I am weak.
I've found a treasure only life can steal;
I've won a jewel only death will keep.
In such a heart as mine, the priceless pearl
Would not be safe. That which I would not take
When health was with me,—which I spurned away
So long as I had power to sin, I fear
Would be surrendered with that power's return
And the temptation to its exercise.
For soul like mine, diseased in every part,

There is but one condition in which grace
May give it service. For my malady
The Great Physician draws the blood away
That only flows to feed its baleful fires;
For only thus the balsam and the balm
May touch the springs of healing.

So I pray
To be delivered from myself,—to be
Delivered from necessity of ill,—
To be secured from bringing harm to you.
Oh, what a boon is death to the sick soul!
I greet it with a joy that passes speech.
Were the whole world to come before me now,—
Wealth with its treasures; Pleasure with its cup;
Power robed in purple; Beauty in its pride,
And with Love's sweetest blossoms garlanded;
Fame with its bays, and Glory with its crown,—
To tempt me lifeward, I would turn away,
And stretch my hands with utter eagerness

Toward the pale angel waiting for me now,
And give my hand to him, to be led out,
Serenely singing, to the land of shade.

MARY.

Edward, I yield you. I would not retain
One who has strayed so long from God and heaven,
When his weak feet have found the only path
Open for such as he.

EDWARD.

My strength recedes;
But ere it fail, tell me how fares your life.
You have seen sorrow ; but it comforts me
To hear the language of a chastened soul
From one perverted by my guilty hand.
You speak the dialect of the redeemed—
The Heaven-accepted. Tell me it is so,
And you are happy.

MARY.

With sweet hope and trust
I may reply, 'tis as you think and wish.
I have seen sorrow, surely, and the more
That I have seen what was far worse; but God
Sent his own servant to me to restore
My sadly straying feet to the sure path;
And in my soul I have the pledge of grace
Which shall suffice to keep them there.

EDWARD.

Ah, joy!
You found a friend; and my o'erflowing heart,
Welling with gratitude, pours out to him
For his kind ministry its fitting meed.
Oh, breathe his name to me, that my poor lips
May bind it to a benison, and that,
While dying, I may whisper it with those—
Jesus and Mary—which I love the best.
Name him, I pray you.

MARY.

You would ask of me
To bear your thanks to him, and to rehearse
Your dying words?

GRACE.

He asks your good friend's name
You do not understand him.

MARY.

It is hard
To give denial to a dying wish;
But, Edward, I've no right to speak his name.
He was a Christian man, and you may give
Of the full largess of your gratitude
All, without robbing God, you have to give,
And fail, e'en then, of worthy recompense.

EDWARD.

Your will is mine.

GRACE.

Nay, Mary, tell it him!
Where is he going he should bruit the name?
Remember where he lies, and that no ears
Save those of angels——

MARY.

There are others here
Who may not hear it.

RUTH.

We will all retire.
It is not proper we should linger here,
Barring the sacred confidence of hearts
Parting so sadly.

DAVID.

Mary, you must yield,
Nor keep the secret longer from your friends.

MARY.

David, you know not what you say.

DAVID.

I know;
So give the dying man no more delay.

MARY

I will declare it under your command.
This stranger friend—stranger for many months—
This man, selectest instrument of Heaven,
Who gave me succor in my hour of need,
Snatched me from ruin, rescued me from want,
Counselled and cheered me, prayed with me, and then
Led me with careful hand into the light,
Was he now bending over you in tears—
David, my brother!

EDWARD.

Blessed be his name!
Brother by every law, above—below!

GRACE.

[*Pale and trembling.*

David? My husband? Did I hear aright?
You are not jesting! Sure you would not jest
At such a juncture! Speak, my husband, speak!
Is this a plot to cheat a dying man,
Or cheat a wife who, if it be no plot,
Is worthy death? What can you mean by this?

MARY.

Not more nor less than my true words convey

GRACE.

Nay, David, tell me!

DAVID.

Mary's words are truth.

GRACE.

O mean and jealous heart, what hast thou done!
What wrong to honor, spite to Christian love,

And shame to self beyond self-pardoning!
How can I ever lift my faithless eyes
To those true eyes that I have counted false;
Or meet those lips that I have charged with lies;
Or win the dear embraces I have spurned?
O most unhappy, most unworthy wife!
No one but he who still has clung to thee,—
Proud, and imperious, and impenitent,—
No one but he who has in silence borne
Thy peevish criminations and complaints
Can now forgive thee, when in deepest shame
Thou bowest with confession of thy faults.
Dear husband! David! Look upon your wife!
Behold one kneeling never knelt to you!
I have abused you and your faithful love,
And, in my great humiliation, pray
You will not trample me beneath your feet.
Pity my weakness, and remember, too,
That Love was jealous of thee, and not Hate—
That it was Love's own pride tormented me.

My husband, take me once more to your arms,
And kiss me in forgiveness; say that you
Will be my counsellor, my friend, my love;
And I will give myself to you again,
To be all yours—my reason, confidence,
My faith and trust all yours, my heart's best love,
My service and my prayers, all yours—all yours!

DAVID.

Rise, dearest, rise! It gives me only pain
That such as you should kneel to such as I.
Your words inform me that you know how weak
I am whom you have only fancied weak.
Forgive you? I forgive you everything;
And take the pardon which your prayer insures.
Let this embrace, this kiss, be evidence
Our jarring hearts catch common rhythm again,
And we are lovers.

RUTH.

Hush! You trouble him.
He understands this scene no more than we.
Mary, he speaks to you.

EDWARD.

Dear wife, farewell!
The room grows dim, and silently and soft
The veil is dropping 'twixt my eyes and yours,
Which soon will hide me from you—you from me.
Only one hand is warm; it rests in yours,
Whose full, sweet pulses throb along my arm,
So that I live upon them. Cling to me!
And thus your life, after my life is past,
Shall lay me gently in the arms of Death.
Thus shall you link your being with a soul
Gazing unveiled upon the Great White Throne.

Dear hearts of love surrounding me, farewell!
I cannot see you now; or, if I do,

You are transfigured. There are floating forms
That whisper over me like summer leaves;
And now there comes, and spreads through all my soul,
Delicious influx of another life,
From out whose essence spring, like living flowers,
Angelic senses with quick ultimates,
That catch the rustle of etherial robes,
And the thin chime of melting minstrelsy—
Rising and falling—answered far away—
As Echo, dreaming in the twilight woods,
Repeats the warble of her twilight birds.
And flowers that mock the Iris toss their cups
In the impulsive ether, and spill out
Sweet tides of perfume, fragrant deluges,
Flooding my spirit like an angel's breath.

* * * * * * *

And still the throng increases; still unfold
With broader span and more elusive sweep
The radiant vistas of a world divine.
But O my soul! what vision rises now!

Far, far away, white blazing like the sun,
In deepest distance and on highest height,
Through walls diaphanous, and atmosphere
Flecked with unnumbered forms of missive power,
Out-going fleetly and returning slow,
A presence shines I may not penetrate;
But on a throne, with smile ineffable,
I see a form my conscious spirit knows.
Jesus, my Saviour! Jesus, Lamb of God!
Jesus who taketh from me all my sins,
And from the world! Jesus, I come to thee!
Come thou to me! O come, Lord, quickly! Come!

DAVID.

Flown on the wings of rapture! Is this death?
His heart is still; his beaded brow is cold;
His wasted breast struggles for breath no more;
And his pale features, hardened with the stress
Of Life's resistance, momently subside
Into a smile, calm as a twilight lake,

Sprent with the images of rising stars.
We have seen Evil in his countless forms
In these poor lives; have met his armed hosts
In dread encounter and discomfiture;
And languished in captivity to them,
Until we lost our courage and our faith;
And here we see their Chieftain—Terror's King!
He cuts the knot that binds a weary soul
To faithless passions, sateless appetites,
And powers perverted, and it flies away
Singing toward Heaven. He turns and looks at us,
And finds us weeping with our gratitude—
Full of sweet sorrow,—sorrow sweeter far
Than the supremest ecstasy of joy.

And this is death! Think you that raptured soul
Now walking humbly in the golden streets,
Bearing the precious burden of a love
Too great for utterance, or with hushed heart
Drinking the music of the ransomed throng,

Counts death an evil?—evil, sickness, pain,
Calamity, or aught that God prescribed
To cure it of its sin, or bring it where
The healing hand of Christ might touch it? No!
He is a man to-night—a man in Christ.
This was his childhood, here; and as we give
A smile of wonder to the little woes
That drew the tears from out our own young eyes
The kind corrections and severe constraints
Imposed by those who loved us—so he sees
A father's chastisement in all the ill
That filled his life with darkness; so he sees
In every evil a kind instrument
To chasten, elevate, correct, subdue,
And fit him for that heavenly estate—
Saintship in Christ—the Manhood Absolute!

L'ENVOY.

Midnight and silence! In the West, unveiled,
The broad, full moon is shining, with the stars.
On mount and valley, forest, roof, and rock,
On billowy hills smooth-stretching to the sky,
On rail and wall, on all things far and near,
Cling the bright crystals,—all the earth a floor
Of polished silver, pranked with bending forms
Uplifting to the light their precious weight
Of pearls and diamonds, set in palest gold.
The storm is dead; and when it rolled away
It took no star from heaven, but left to earth
Such legacy of beauty as The Wind—
The light-robed shepherdess from Cuban groves—
Driving soft showers before her, and warm airs,
And her wide-scattered flocks of wet-winged birds,

Never bestowed upon the waiting Spring.
Pale, silent, smiling, cold, and beautiful!
Do storms die thus? And is it this to die?

Midnight and silence! In that hallowed room
God's full-orbed peace is shining, with the stars.
On head and hand, on brow, and lip, and eye,
On folded arms, on broad unmoving breast,
On the white-sanded floor, on everything,
Rests the pale radiance, while bending forms
Stand all around, loaded with precious weight
Of jewels such as holy angels wear.
The man is dead; and when he passed away
He blotted out no good, but left behind
Such wealth of faith, such store of love and trust,
As breath of joy, in-floating from the isles
Smiled on by ceaseless summer, and indued
With foliage and flowers perennial,
Never conveyed to the enchanted soul.
Do men die thus? And is it this to die?

Midnight and silence! At each waiting bed,
Husband and wife, embracing, kneel in prayer;
And lips unused to such a benison
Breathe blessings upon evil, and give thanks
For knowledge of its sacred ministry.
An infant nestles on a mother's breast,
Whose head is pillowed where it has not lain
For months of wasted life—the tale all told,
And confidence and love for-aye secure

The widow and the virgin: where are they?
The morn shall find them watching with the dead,
Like the two angels at the tomb of Christ,—
One at the head, the other at the foot,—
Guarding a sepulchre whose occupant
Has risen, and rolled the heavy stone away!

THE END.

www.ingramcontent.com/pod-product-compliance
Lightning Source LLC
LaVergne TN
LVHW011206110826
845150LV00006B/1334

9781425517922